D1410176

SWEET TEA
for the
SOUL

COMFORTING,
REAL-LIFE STORIES
FOR

Moms

DaySpring
LIVE YOUR FAITH

Sweet Tea for the Soul: Comforting, Real-Life Stories for Moms
Copyright © 2021 DaySpring Cards, Inc. All rights reserved.
First Edition, March 2021

Published by:

21154 Highway 16 East
Siloam Springs, AR 72761
dayspring.com

Produced with the assistance of Peachtree Publishing Services
Design by: Jessica Wei

Printed in China
Prime: J3110
ISBN: 978-1-64454-847-9

Contents

Not One More! 7

Beautiful Shipwreck 11

Splash Park Showdown 15

The Knock 19

Beauty in the Mess 23

Edge of the Mat 27

The Real Picture 31

Confident You 35

It's That Simple 40

Open Arms 44

Blended Life 48

Stained Glass Life 52

Digging Holes 56

Playtime Wins 60

This Is the Way 64

When Reality Rules 68

Rinse and Repeat 72

Got Regret? 76

The Best Happy 80

Hands-Off Connection 84

Contentment Within 89

I Want That Baby, Diego 93

A Child Like Peter 97

Chaos at Its Finest 101

Hide-and-Seek 106

The Loser Mom Club. 110

Spirited Sprouts 114

Cheese Sauce. 118

One of Those Days 122

The Value of Other Mamas 126

Give Me That Mountain 130

Seen and Loved 133

Upside-Down Map. 137

Carefree or in Control?. 141

You Are Mine. 145

A Little More Time 149

Maybe Later. 153

The Superpower of Rest 156

What's Really Needed 160

Grace When We Forget. 164

Promises, Promises 168

Stuff Happens. 172

Rejoicing in the Mess 176

Giver of All Good Things 180

No Kidding. 184

Chocolate for Breakfast. 189

When You Don't Know What to Do 193

Embracing the Mess. 197

The Heart's Desires. 201

Kitty Litter Confetti. 204

Not One More!

*"[God] never responds with 'not one more' when I am
in need of Him lavishing love on my thirsty heart,
forgiving my sin, or pouring peace into my unquiet soul."*

Ever feel like you just cannot do "one more"? Not one more meal. Not one more diaper. Not one more poster board for a high schooler's homework assignment. Not one more *Daniel Tiger's Neighborhood*. Not one more spill to clean up.

Not long ago, I was having one of those not-one-more moments. The laundry was piled up higher than normal, and there were still so many things left to do. But I just could not bring myself to do one more thing that day—especially not one more load of laundry!

However, the next morning, our family was in our typical mode of rushing to get out the door for school and work. It was a flurry of throwing together breakfast and lunches, shoving homework into backpacks, clamoring about after-school activities, and solidifying the evening schedule.

During that perfect-storm moment our not-yet-dressed teenage daughter raised her voice and declared she "just had to have" a specific white tank top before she could get dressed. Of course, the said tank top could not be found, and the only place left to look was the pile of dirty laundry. In her mind, no other tank top would do, not even another white one.

With no other choice, we went searching through the

laundry and found the beloved tank top. It was in a damp, wrinkled ball at the bottom of the laundry basket, under a massive pile of smelly, dirty clothes. Looking my daughter in the eye, I thought this would surely change her mind about needing this particular tank top—but I was wrong.

"That's the one!" she said. And I agreed with her—it was the one. It was the one in need of laundering, maybe even twice! But to her, it was the one she *had* to wear that day.

Trying to come up with a solution to this laundry dilemma, I spotted a bottle of Febreze. Never before had so much been required of a laundry aid. I sprayed that white tank top every which way, inside and out. I drenched it in the extra-strength fabric refresher that promised to eliminate lingering odors. My daughter quickly put it on under the rest of her darling outfit, and out the door she went.

Left in a fog of Febreze, I felt remorse about not having done one more load of laundry the night before. I was in tears, not feeling like a good mom, and my doubts were mounting about the efficacy of said fabric refresher. (Does it truly eliminate damp, smelly, lingering odors?)

At the same time, I had an awareness come over me of God's nearness. I needed Him. Even standing over that pile of dirty laundry, I needed to know that God's unconditional love surrounded me. As my inner voice was railing about my failure as a mom, having let that one more thing pile up, the still, small voice of our loving Jesus soothed me with the truth. I realized then that I am not a bad mom because I sent my daughter to school in a good-smelling yet filthy article of clothing. I am a good mom who adjusted my standards of cleanliness (which is *not* really next to godliness) and helped my daughter go to school in the clothes she felt confident wearing.

Hundreds of times I have been in that space of self-doubt, hearing a negative inner voice, feeling like a failure, and needing God's assurance of love. I am deeply grateful that our heavenly Father never says "not one more" to us. He never responds with "not one more" when I need Him to lavish His love on my thirsty heart, forgive my sin, or pour peace into my unquiet soul. God never withholds His good stuff; He always offers *more*. He rains down; I soak up. His supply is always fresh and never-ending.

One of my mentors taught me something interesting about divine supply and demand. As we go to our divine God with our needs—and sometimes our demands—we let Him know every need, big or small. Then, in His divine supply nature, He gives us *exactly* what we need for that moment and situation.

Interestingly, the divine nature of God's supply is twofold. First, His divine ways are so much better than ours. His kindness, creativity, and patience are infinitely superior to anything we could possibly offer. Second, when we go back to God with our next need or demand, the quantity (and dare I say quality) of His divine resources have not diminished at all! It's as if we've never asked anything of Him before.

Consider how that would look if this kind of divine supply happened with ice cream. We would open the quart, scoop out as much ice cream as the bowl could handle, and enjoy every spoonful. The next day (or later that day if I'm being totally honest), we would open the same container and find it full to the brim with a smooth surface of ice cream—divine supply indeed!

Though God's supply is divine, that's not the way it is with us humans. We easily come to the end of ourselves—especially as moms. Because much is required of us, we desire to be and give and do, all to take care of those we love. Am I right?

But in our humanity, we often reach that "not one more" feeling. Not one more pan of brownies for a bake sale, not one more conversation about Legos, and not one more week of menus. Those are the times we must rely on the divine supply of God. Even when we do not have one more thing to give at the end of a draining day, God always has what we need.

Ephesians 3:19 says, "May you experience the love of Christ, though it is too great to understand fully. Then you will be made complete with all the fullness of life and power that comes from God" (NLT).

The love of Christ can flow through us to read that storybook one more time or drive one more group of noisy kiddos to practice. Christ's love—too great to understand fully—is more than enough! And when we come to the end of ourselves, where the life and power of Jesus take over, He divinely supplies the very next thing we need.

It's true—we often do not have it in us to do one more thing. Equally true is that we *do* have the Spirit of God to do one more thing through us. I don't know about you, but I am trying to more readily tap into that divine, never-ending, fresh resource and supply of Jesus. I am also trying to embrace and smile at the imperfections of life. My hope and prayer are that you will too.

—JILL ST. JOHN, LEE'S SUMMIT, MISSOURI

Beautiful Shipwreck

*"If there's anyone who is patient with big messes
being made in the harvest, it's our heavenly Father.
He consistently extends grace to us,
right in the middle of our messes,
and responds kindly to us time and time again."*

I have four children. (Need I say more?) Their ages are fourteen, twelve, six, and five. And while I'd love to say that things are always smooth sailing, in reality, I run a tight shipwreck.

As a working mom, life is so much easier when things are clean and organized and everyone gets along. But that only happens about every March 32nd. Can you relate?

Don't you sometimes wish you could be like Cinderella's fairy godmother and wave a magic wand? With a simple "bibbidi-bobbidi-boo," you'd open your eyes to find that all of life's messes were magically clean and as shiny as a glass slipper.

When my daughter was two years old, my husband had called and asked if we could have his boss over at the last minute. "Sure, sweetie," I said through a pasted smile and clenched teeth. "No problem at all!"

I hung up the phone with ninety-four things on my to-do list, including cleaning the house top to bottom, making a yummy meal, and hopefully brushing my hair before said boss arrived. No problem, right? Rush. Rush. Rush. Clean. Brush hair. Clean some more. (Oh, and make something decent for dinner!)

Needless to say, my day became a harried frenzy to get it all done. And just as I had finished cleaning, ready to head upstairs to make myself presentable, I looked in the dining room and saw little white fluffy things stuck to the walls. What on earth?

I got closer and realized it was bits of dried toilet paper! Stuck. To. The. Walls. My sweet two-year-old came waltzing out of the bathroom with another wad of wet toilet paper (please don't ask how it got wet) and proceeded to stick it to the wall!

With a half-crazed look in my eye, I frantically asked, "What are you *doing*? I *just* got the house clean. Why would you do this?"

I will never forget the crushed look on her face. In the saddest, most pathetic way, she started to cry and said, "Momma, I was hepping you keen. I sowy."

Oh. My. Stars.

Instantly, I became the one with the sad face and broken heart, and *I* started to cry. How could I have responded to her this way? I had been more worried about my house being perfectly clean than I was about her beautiful little heart. I was devastated at how I had responded. I sat on the floor, told her I was sorry for not being patient with her, and told her how thankful I was that she was willing to help Momma clean.

I'd love to say that it was the last time I responded like that toward my children, that I learned my lesson right then and there, that I welcomed messes and recognized the bigger picture of what was transpiring. But that's not the case. Over the years, I have responded impatiently more times than I can count. I have been more concerned with the messes being made than the memories being formed.

I would love to say that I always live for the beauty of the moment, but I struggle to slow down long enough to do this. As someone who likes her house clean and organized, it's easier to say no more often than to say yes. But I'm so thankful for God's grace and patience with me through this thing called motherhood. My daily prayer is that He will fill me to overflowing with the same grace and patience toward each of my children.

Proverbs 14:4 has literally revolutionized the way I parent. It's a verse I've read countless times in my life, but I never really understood or connected with it until a few years ago. It says, "Without oxen a stable stays clean, but you need a strong ox for a large harvest" (NLT).

One day, I came across that verse again, and all of a sudden it clicked! It finally made sense. If I wanted a large harvest—a beautiful, fulfilling life with my family—I would need a big ox (and the mess that comes with it).

The truth is, I want a large harvest! I want my children to grow up learning new things, laughing along the way, creating memories, and feeling peace and joy in their home. But if I'm so strict and controlling about messes, structure, and order, I'll diminish these experiences for them.

While I'm someone who thrives on crossing things off my to-do list, I'm slowly learning to be more concerned about the memories than the messes being made. I am learning to create a peaceful environment where joy and laughter are plentiful, where things aren't so uptight, and where *I'm* not so uptight. Sometimes when my husband and I look around the house, we joke, "It looks like it's been a 'big ox' kind of a day!"

If you're anything like me and have the tendency to dwell on your faults and shortcomings, I encourage you to *stop*!

Stop picking yourself apart. Stop beating yourself up for the ways you fall short. Be reminded today of God's beautiful grace and kindness toward you—right where you are—in your beautiful shipwreck called "life."

If there's anyone who is patient with big messes being made in the harvest, it's our heavenly Father. He consistently extends grace to us, right in the middle of our messes, and responds kindly to us time and time again. Let's allow His patience and kindness to be what mark us as women and as mothers.

—JAMIE JONES, NUNICA, MICHIGAN

Splash Park Showdown

*"My response in the next few moments
would serve as an example for my daughter.
I realized I needed to teach conflict resolution
with mercy, respect, and integrity."*

We had a brawl at the splash park today. Well, it wasn't really a brawl, per se, but both mothers involved went into defensive positions for sure. It was one of those priceless teachable moments that could have seriously gone off the rails. I was faced with an instant decision: handle the issue either out of anger or with integrity and respect— something that can put out a fire and leave an indelible impression.

It was 102 degrees (in the shade) on an ordinary Tennessee day. Unfortunately, the pool was closed, so we headed to the splash park. I hardly knew anyone there, so I staked out a table and sat down to read a book alone. I hadn't been reading too long when my oldest daughter, Adrienne, stomped up to me with her long, tan legs.

"Some lady just stole my water gun right out of my hand and marched off with it," she said. "She told me I could have it back when I learned to stop spraying people in the face."

Confusion. Embarrassment. Irritation. Defensiveness. All of these emotions swirled at once, threatening to cloud godly judgment. No, Adrienne should not have been spraying strangers in the face. We'd had this conversation before, and I knew she was well aware of the rules. Still, she shouldn't be treated like a villain for being a regular kid at a splash park!

Part of me wanted to shrug it off as if it didn't matter. And truthfully, that would have been the easy road. I could have told her to find something else to do and gone back to reading my book. However, that would send Adrienne the message that she wasn't worth it to me, or that the lady's strong opinion of her was true. I quickly realized that my response in the next few moments would serve as an example for my daughter. I realized I needed to teach conflict resolution with mercy, respect, and integrity.

As I stood up, I instinctively knew we were being watched. With my heart pounding I said to Adrienne, "Keep in mind that people are imperfect, and they all have their own reasons for what they do. We can only do our best and assume that everyone else is doing their best too. It's going to be okay."

I felt the Holy Spirit guiding my response in a way that would teach Adrienne to lead with love, set healthy boundaries, and still treat others with integrity.

"Come on, let's go get your water gun back," I said, taking a deep breath. We walked over to the woman and stopped in front of her. I leaned in to gently take the water gun back and spoke in a quiet, measured voice—loud enough for only the three of us to hear. "We're sorry for the offense, but my daughter, Adrienne, was just being a kid and didn't notice she was offending people. She's actually a good girl. All you have to do is ask her to stop and she will obey."

Toy in hand and daughter in tow, I slipped away calmly. A few moments later, after I had retreated to my seat and was pretending to read, the lady approached me. I peered up at her, bracing for impact. However, she surprised me with her words.

"I'm sorry," she began. "You're right. I overreacted. She

was spraying my daughter, who has special needs, and it made me mad. But you were so kind and calm, it made me realize my overreaction."

It was an "aha" moment for me. The woman wasn't just a mean lady at the splash park; she was a mother. Her job had undoubtedly been harder than mine, and it was obvious her reserves had been exhausted.

I realized our unique roles in motherhood drove each of our actions that day, causing us to step beyond our comfort zones and do what needed to be done. She didn't have to apologize, but the fact that she did spoke volumes to me about her character.

I didn't give her my name, but I did give her my best effort, thanks to the Holy Spirit. And while I couldn't see behind her sunglasses, I did see into her heart. In that moment, I was so thankful I had shown her the respect she deserved and modeled that for my daughter. And what I felt in return was empathy, camaraderie, and admiration.

That splash park experience reminds me of a Bible passage: "Finally, all of you, be like-minded, be sympathetic, love one another, be compassionate and humble. Do not repay evil with evil or insult with insult. On the contrary, repay evil with blessing, because to this you were called so that you may inherit a blessing" (I PETER 3:8–9 NIV).

Many different scenarios could have unfolded that day—many I would have regretted. But by the prompting of the Holy Spirit to be the best example to my daughter that I could be, I did the hard thing by remaining calm and respectful.

If you're like me, someone who finds it tempting to react instead of respond, I encourage you to take a moment to gather your initial brawl-like thoughts and allow the Lord to speak peace over the situation. Then, do the hard thing by leading with integrity and respect. It can make all the difference in the world!

—MELISSA BRENDTRO, PENSACOLA, FLORIDA

The Knock

*"Our kids don't always know
what's going on in our lives.
They don't know the pressures we're under
in our jobs or ministries."*

The knock wasn't loud, but it was firm and authoritative. And honestly, it couldn't have come at a worse time. I was cooking for a ministry group that would be arriving later that evening and staying with us for five nights. As the wife of a pastor of a small church, we often housed traveling groups that came through.

On that particular day, we were right in the middle of a three-week revival, with almost nightly meetings. Not only that, but I was also sick. So very sick. It had started as allergies and had quickly morphed into something much worse. My head felt like it weighed a thousand pounds. I had a fever, and I could barely breathe. Later, I would learn that I had a severe case of bronchitis, which would require steroids to cure. But I didn't know any of this at that time.

All I knew was that I was late getting dinner started, our new guests were expected to arrive any minute, and the house was a mess. I felt like death, and the kids were being, well, kids. With a teenage daughter, two small sons, and an international student spending the year with us, I certainly had my hands full. And because my hubby was gone a lot tending to all the "irons in the fire," I was pretty much on my own to prepare for our guests—if and when they arrived.

So, getting back to the knock—that untimely knock on the door—I asked my daughter to answer it. Moments later, she came to get me. "Mom, you need to come here," she said in a serious tone.

Thinking it was our new guests, I told her to let them in and I'd be right there once I finished browning the meat. However, she stood firmly in the kitchen doorway. "No, Mom. You gotta come now."

I looked at her, annoyed. She and I had been finding ourselves at an almost constant impasse. Anything I asked of her was usually met with assorted noises of displeasure or questions such as "Why Mom? How come? Do I have to do that right now?" I was *really* not in the mood to deal with it, so I said snappily, "Just let them in and tell them I'll be right out."

With anxiousness in her voice, she said, "Mom, it's the police."

What! I poked my head around our kitchen entryway and saw a police officer standing on our front step. *Yikes! What on earth?* I thought. Quickly removing the frying pan from the burner, I wiped my hands and went to the front door.

"Hello, Officer," I said, as calmly as I could. "Can I help you?"

"Good evening, ma'am. Are these your boys?"

That's when I noticed our two sons standing behind the officer as nonchalantly as five- and six-year-old-boys could. They had their hands behind their backs and eyes looking skyward. If they could have whistled, they would have.

At that moment, I was tempted to shake my head and say, "Nope, never saw them before in my life." But as our six-year-old briefly caught my eye, I saw his fear and uncertainty, and I decided I just couldn't do it. Besides, this officer didn't look like the type who would appreciate the joke.

"Yes, those are my boys," I answered.

"Do you know where they were just now?" he asked.

"Well," I said, glaring at them, "they better have been in the front yard since they had strict instructions to play there."

"Well, ma'am," the officer said, "I found them down by the stop sign over there." He pointed to the end of our road. "They were throwing empty soda bottles at cars."

A construction company had been building homes in our area and had left lots of assorted trash at the site, including empty soda bottles. While I heard what the officer was saying, my mind was slow to take it in.

"Who. . . what. . . where were they?" I stuttered.

The officer repeated himself and then half smiled when he saw my face. "So, is it fair to assume this will be handled properly?"

"Oh, yes, Officer," I replied, as invisible steam slowly started pouring out of my ears (just like a cartoon character).

"I'll be calling their father to handle it," I said as calmly as possible. (I wasn't in the right frame of mind to handle anything!)

Satisfied that it would be taken care of, and perhaps wondering if he'd be back later to collect two small bodies, the officer turned to the boys and said sternly, "Never throw things at cars again. Understand?"

"Yes, sir!" both boys earnestly replied.

Silently, the boys walked into the house. At this point, I was glad our guests were running late. I was furious! How could my boys have done this? Didn't they know the pressure I was under? Didn't they know how sick I was? Didn't they know how much I had to do?

Of course they didn't. They were two little boys having fun, not realizing the consequences. I bet they didn't even realize how far the stop sign was from the front yard. I immediately called their dad and relayed the story to him. The boys were properly chastised and trained on the impracticality, let alone the danger, of throwing things at cars. Our guests arrived, and eventually I got medication to quell my aching head and chest.

The thing is, our kids don't always know what's going on in our lives. They don't know the pressures we're under in our jobs or ministries. And while we get caught up in the demands of life as an adult, it would be good to remember that our biggest ministry is our children.

Jesus reminded His disciples of the importance of little ones when He said, "Whoever receives one such child in my name receives me, and whoever receives me, receives not me but him who sent me" (MARK 9:37 ESV).

Our children see the good, bad, and ugly in us. And how we respond to situations will stick with them for the rest of their lives. They'll even pass those memories to their own children. So the big question for us is, what do we want our grandchildren to hear about us?

A few days later, we were talking about the police incident, and my husband and I wondered how the police officer knew the boys were throwing the bottles. That's when our youngest piped up and said, "It was probably when we hit his windshield with one of them!" Of course it was.

—TRACY O'BRIEN, KANSAS CITY, MISSOURI

Beauty in the Mess

"It's easy to want others to see us as put-together women. But God is far less concerned with the show we put on and far more concerned with what is happening in our hearts."

The first time I entered the home of my daughter's friend, I felt uncomfortable and embarrassed. The mother, who had just returned from running errands around town, wore pressed pants and a crisp button-down top.

On the other hand, I looked like I had just crawled out of a cave.

I'd just finished a hike in the woods. But to be real with you, even if I'd been out running errands, I still would have worn the same cut-off sweatpants, running sneakers, and long-sleeve athletic top. Add to that my messy, windblown wisps of hair escaping my hair tie and the essence of dirt hanging around me—I looked like I'd just been swept in by the Dust Bowl!

Standing in the doorway of that gorgeous house that far exceeded my family's financial means, I looked down to see my sweet daughters with new eyes. My middle child had a huge brown patch of dirt on her shirt. Her hair was in a ratty ponytail that looked as if she hadn't brushed it for days. My youngest sported dirt-caked jeans, filthy hands, smudged glasses, and dirt around her mouth—around *her mouth*! (How does that even happen?)

I chatted with the mother as if we were both part of the same pristine world, but I cringed inside about how insanely messy and not put together my little family was. To add insult to injury, I thought about a time earlier in the week, when the father from this same family had picked his daughter up from our home. He had walked in immediately after our church plant's pre-launch party, where we'd opened dozens of boxes of equipment that had arrived. Picture about forty empty cardboard boxes and their packing materials scattered throughout the main living area of my home. Everything a church could need sat in piles and stacks around my house. I remember being mildly embarrassed at the time, but I'd also patted myself on the back for not letting it bother me too much. I thought I had come so far in learning to give myself grace and live transparently. But upon stepping into *their* home with our earth-covered shoes and ratty ponytails, all thoughts of letting go of perfectionism went up in a cloud of dust—literally (think Pigpen from the comic strip *Peanuts*).

Before entering that beautiful home, I had a completely different perception of myself and my girls. I saw myself as providing a fun, healthy, and carefree day for my kids. Watching my daughters as they climbed rocks and trees, walked with arms draped across each other's shoulders, and gave piggyback rides to my neighbor's kids was to me a picture of perfection. During our afternoon of sunshine and laughter, I didn't even notice smudged glasses or dirt-stained shirts. But once I stepped into that put-together world without a trace of dust, my ego rose up and altered my perspective.

Later, as I recounted the experience to a friend, I couldn't help but laugh hysterically. What else was there to do? In reality, this is me and this is my world. My home is disassembled and put back together again every couple of days as we use it as a staging ground for a church where the messiest of people are welcome. My schedule doesn't leave a lot of room for both quality time with the kids and a visit to the nail salon, so I try to choose what's most important.

Trust me, I know it's easy to want others to see us as put-together women. But God is far less concerned with the show we put on and far more concerned with what is happening in our hearts. In general, we women put a lot of time and energy into controlling other's perceptions of us—which wears us out in the process. But again, God is far more concerned with the condition of our hearts.

First Samuel 16:7 says, "But the LORD said to Samuel, 'Don't judge by his appearance or height, for I have rejected him. The LORD doesn't see things the way you see them. People judge by outward appearance, but the LORD looks at the heart'" (NLT).

God looks at us the way I looked at my daughters before I stepped into that perfect home. He isn't repulsed by our disorganization or our imperfections, nor is He impressed by the image we strive to present to the world. He looks deeper within. He knows His daughters and He sees our beauty in the mess. Never does He ask us to wear ourselves out and work harder to become perfect. Instead, He calls us to surrender. And as we do, He provides the cleansing and righteousness through His Son.

Our God is willing to do the hard work for us. All He asks is that we lay ourselves bare and transparent before Him and accept His healing love. So bring your windblown hair and dirt-stained shirts (or faces), and rest in the presence of the One who knows you and loves you. Try to view things as He views them, and find beauty in the mess. And while you're at it, don't forget to invite over the mother who looks like she stepped out of *Vogue* or *Good Housekeeping*, because she could probably use a little love and acceptance too.

—REBECCA BURTRAM, CHARLOTTESVILLE, VIRGINIA

Edge of the Mat

*"As our kids grow and change,
training them to listen to our voice is important,
but that pales in comparison to training them
to listen to the voice of their Coach."*

If you've never been a wrestling mom, I have to tell you, it's a weird little sport. It's loud and chaotic and a bit hard to figure out. Tiny gladiators step onto the mats in their strange uniforms, shake hands, and then try to pin their opponent—all the while earning points for various moves. It took me over a year to figure out what the different moves mean and how the point system works.

But once I did, I was *that* mom! I was the mom packing a cooler full of sandwiches, carrot sticks, fruit, and water bottles. I'd leave the house at "o'dark thirty" to spend all day in a noisy, smelly gym to cheer for my tiny gladiator. I was even the mom who was recorded on camera yelling, "Joshua, I did *not* get up at 4:00 a.m. to watch you lose. Get out of that hold!"

For eight full years my boy wrestled, and twice, he even placed at the New York State Championship! It was a fun and exciting season for all of us. And as we got to know the other wrestling families, we formed a support system where sportsmanship and kindness were held in high regard. Every wrestler, no matter their age, was expected to handle wins and losses with dignity and respect.

But even more important than sportsmanship, one

person at every match matters most—the coach. He knows his wrestlers well. He knows the strengths and weaknesses of every kid. And he often knows the same about their opponents. The coach perches on his knees at the edge of the mat, watches every move, and anticipates his wrestler's countermoves. He can foresee all the possible outcomes.

The wrestler must *listen* to the coach. There are a whole lot of voices clamoring in those gyms with multiple matches, lots of parents, and even more kids. It's a cacophony of chaos. And the wrestler is at a disadvantage due to the noise, upside-down holds, and limited field of vision. He *needs* the coach.

The coach directs the wrestler throughout the entire match, telling him what to do and what to avoid. He says things like "No! Half! Drive! Get your head out!" These commands direct the wrestler to the next hold, counter-move, or escape. And above all other voices, the coach's is most important.

One weekend, we walked into a typical tournament, weighed our son in, and waited to see who he would be wrestling. When we found out he would go up against a multiple-time state champion, my heart sank. I had never seen this boy lose! He was strong, well trained, and seasoned. And I was worried.

I stood on the edge of the mat and waited to see what would happen. My husband, our son's coach, knelt in the corner. The referee blew his whistle and the match began.

After the first round, the boys were tied. A crowd had started to gather around. None of the people were part of our wrestling club or the club of our opponent. But they knew the state champ well, and many of them knew our son.

Calmly and clearly the coach called out, "Get out of that!

Get to your base! Turn!" I was silent, as I had no business getting involved. My son did not focus on the crowd, the noise, or even his opponent. He concentrated on the voice of the coach he trusted—his father—who knew him, had studied his opponent's moves, and would direct him through the match.

Round two ended with my son ahead by two points. I couldn't breathe. Several of our friends stood with me, and one of them grabbed my shaking hand. I almost wished my son would get pinned so I could exhale. But round three started as the whistle blew.

Honestly, it felt like round three took about thirty-seven years! Surprisingly, the crowd wasn't noisy. I could clearly hear the coach telling my boy what to do next. At the end of round three the boys were tied. The match went into overtime and the state champ finally won. But it didn't matter. I had never been prouder of how my son wrestled. When the boys shook hands, they threw their arms around each other and acknowledged the difficulty and drain of the moment.

I watched as families surrounded the boys and shook my son's hand. Like me, they saw in him the focus and determination of a good wrestler and the ability to allow his coach to direct him in a match that should have been over in the first round. It was incredible.

Why would I tell you about a match my son lost? Because the story is less about the boy and more about the coach. As our kids grow and change, training them to listen to our voice is important, but that pales in comparison to training them to listen to the voice of their Coach. In a confusing and chaotic culture, whose voice should they focus on? Like the wrestler, our children must learn to tune out all the distractions and zero in on the one voice that matters most—the voice of their Father.

Jesus said, "My sheep listen to My voice; I know them, and they follow Me. I give them eternal life, and they shall never perish; no one will snatch them out of My hand" (JOHN 10:27–28 NIV).

Our parenting goal should not be to replicate our ideas, thoughts, and opinions in our child. Our goal should be to help our children develop ears and hearts that listen to the voice of their Shepherd. After all, when the noise of life and the chaos of trouble comes and we can only stand helplessly on the edge of the mat, whose voice do we want them to hear?

—LISA DURANT, BREWERTON, NEW YORK

The Real Picture

*"God has never wanted to be a passive presence
in our lives. He wants to talk out our problems
and decisions with us. He wants companionship,
and keeping a safe distance simply won't do."*

No one sells a bill of goods on motherhood quite like
the Labor and Delivery Department. As you walk
through the halls and look at pictures of beautiful
moms-to-be, smiling parents, and peacefully sleeping babies,
you think to yourself, *Yes, I'd like one of those, please.*

Who wouldn't? Those images make motherhood seem
like a dream come true! But you know what, girl? Peacefully
sleeping babies and pretty moms smiling at adoring husbands
are all a dream! Where are the pictures of cankles, screaming
babies at 2:00 a.m., and prenatal acne? Let's hang some real-
life portraits of hemorrhoid cream and nursing bras on
those Labor and Delivery walls! (Can I get an amen?)

I don't think anything in life is more beautifully awkward
than motherhood. From my own experience, having four
little munchkins within a span of seven years, I was either
lactating or pregnant for the first decade of my marriage.
Though my husband and I didn't really plan to build our
family that quickly, we loved every awkward, poop-covered,
exhausting minute of it.

The funny thing is, I had never changed a diaper before
my firstborn squalled his way into our lives. God bless those
Labor and Delivery nurses! They changed him for me during

those first few days. My first diaper-changing experience was when he was three days old, and only then because we were being discharged from the hospital. My husband actually had to teach me how to do the diaper thing, along with other ins and outs of babydom. I'd never felt more ill-equipped or ill-prepared for anything in my whole life!

As I was still fumbling and bumbling through my first months as a mom, I discovered I was pregnant—again. My first child was only eight months old! A month before our second baby was due, we decided it was a good time to take a family vacation—requiring a twelve-hour car trip. What were we thinking?

We owned a tiny two-door Honda Civic. Both the driver's and passenger's seats needed to be pushed as far forward as they would go in order for the baby seat to fit in the back. Our son's little head was right in the middle between our shoulders.

Being the overly organized one in the family, I packed our tiny car with more thought and consideration than should ever be given to loading a car. Meticulously, I stacked and packed that little car with beach supplies, food, clothes, and all the baby things (including the cure-all of infancy—pacifiers), and off we went. This was going to be a fun, relaxing, trip—or so I told myself.

A few hours into the trip, we drove over a bump in the road. That despicable bump seemed innocent enough. After all, we'd driven over thousands of them in our lifetime. *That* one, though, was a turning point in our blissful trip. As we drove over that unholy hazard, it caused everything in our trunk to shift. And that tiny movement started a grueling, repetitive tune of the ABCs.

One of my son's favorite toys was a cute, plushy dog

that played different children's songs, depending on which body part you squeezed—and it was stuffed in the bottom of the trunk. That bump we drove over caused that "cute" plushy dog to get stuck on the ABCs in the loudest, most obnoxious way. In a car as small as ours, you could hear every single note as if it was right next to you! That thing played nonstop the rest of the trip. The only way to shut it up was to completely unpack the car, and there was no way we were going to take the time to do that.

After a trillion choruses of the ABCs, we finally arrived at the beach. The first thing we did after unpacking was to remove the batteries from said plushy dog. Whenever our son pushed a button, we blinked innocently and acted like we had no idea why it wouldn't work. (Be honest. I know you've done it too.)

I learned a few lessons on that trip—the most important one being my tendency to live independently from God. In my insecurities of motherhood, I'd overcompensated by trying to organize and control everything. Yet, one bump in the road shifted all my best-laid plans. I'd forgotten that in all my planning, what I needed most was wisdom and guidance from God.

Isaiah 53:6 says, "We're all like sheep who've wandered off and gotten lost. We've all done our own thing, gone our own way. And GOD has piled all our sins, everything we've done wrong, on Him" (THE MESSAGE).

God has never wanted to be a passive presence in our lives. He wants to talk out our problems and decisions with us. He wants *companionship*, and keeping a safe distance simply won't do.

As the child who always wanted to know what was going to happen next, I thought that if I could organize, control, and plan everything, I'd feel safer. I tried hard to keep a safe distance from uncertainty and unpredictability. That way, I didn't need God and His advice.

That's exactly what I did on our vacation. I felt incompetent and insecure about the unknowns of motherhood, and I sought ways to pacify that feeling without God. I should have turned to the Lord in my insecurity and been honest with Him.

I've come to realize there's something fantastic about a prayer that says, "God, I really stink at this. How have You been able to parent so many people with so many issues? Will You teach me?"

Will You teach me?

What a simple yet powerful prayer for us as mothers. We cling to our security blankets of self-sufficiency and independence yet hesitate to simply ask for some much-needed help.

Moms, let's have a heart-to-heart with God. It's time to stop glorifying our overly organized ways as virtues and face the facts of insecurity. Let's allow God to teach us how to be a great parent like Him.

And let's remove all the batteries from those obnoxious toys.

—SARAH KEITH, LEWISBURG, TENNESSEE

Confident You

*"If God is confident in what He is doing in you
and will not stop working in you,
then you had better not give up on yourself."*

Mom. It's a name we love, a name we long for, and a name we hear over and over until it drives us crazy. It's a name we sometimes measure up to and a name we fall short of—often simultaneously.

I frequently think about the Proverbs 31 woman, whom I call "Madge." I've labeled her this way because I think she must be a figment of the imagination of the author. Just reading about her intimidates me and keeps me in the "falling short" category. I mean, who could do all those things and be excellent in them all? For example, her kids "arise and call her blessed" (v. 28 NIV). My kids rise and call me the "Wicked Witch of the West." I sometimes think my epitaph will read, "Here lies Old Yeller" or "Ding, dong the witch is dead."

Can anyone relate?

As a young mom, I struggled to achieve balance. My heart said, "I would rather sit and play a game with my kids than stand at the sink or vacuum." I tried my best to instill disciplines into their lives such as making the bed, washing the dishes, and having a heart to help. However, as a self-described creative and organizationally challenged person, I often failed miserably. This led me to comparing myself to my ultra-organized, house-always-clean friends.

One discipline in which I did succeed, however, was teaching my kids to do laundry—sort of. One day when my son was eleven and my daughter was four, I put clean clothes on the dining room table and told the kids to fold and put them away while I jumped in the shower. I was only in the shower for ten minutes when I smelled something burning. Quickly, I threw on my robe and ran to the dining room. There, hanging from the chandelier were my daughter's panties, smoldering and ready to burst into flames!

Now, I would like to say I laughed out loud and calmly said, "You silly kids. What on earth happened here?" But instead, I reacted out of fear. My Old-Yeller volume was turned up to max capacity, and I could almost envision myself sweeping in on a broomstick cackling, "Who threw the panties on the chandelier, my pretties?"

Seriously, my mind went to the worst-case scenario as I realized my house was about to catch on fire. I could see the news headlines in my mind: "Mom leaves kids alone for ten minutes while they catch the house on fire. This mom is a loser and deserves to be put away."

Needless to say, I sprang into action. I grabbed the now-sparking panties off the light fixture, all the while yelling in my "outside" voice, "WHAT IN THE WORLD WERE YOU GUYS DOING?" Sheepishly, my son answered, "I picked up Brianna's panties and said, 'I am not folding these!' Then I threw them up in the air and they landed on the light. We didn't know they would catch on fire! Honest, Mom!"

In agreement with her brother, my daughter piped up and said, "Yeah, Mommy! That's the troof."

My kids were holding back nervous laughter, but the fear in their eyes was obvious. And at that moment, I had a choice. I could punish them for their panty-burning fiasco or calm down and laugh at the innocent mishap. After a short pause of deliberation, I chose the latter. And boy, am I glad I did! After all, I knew the hearts of my kids were not to catch the house on fire. Pausing to see the situation through my kids' eyes shifted my thinking. I continued to grow into that mindset and thought I was home free.

Wrong. Fast forward several years, and suddenly, the Wicked Witch of the West was back with vengeance. I still think the Lord must have had a sense of humor to give me a sixteen-year-old daughter just as I was entering menopause. (Thankfully, my son was already at college and away from my cackling mood swings.) The joy-squashing comparison trap baited me once again, and I berated myself. Only this time it teamed up with social media, screaming in my face, "You don't measure up!"

One day I was searching the Scriptures for an encouragement to set me free from the comparison. Guess where the Lord took me? Proverbs 31. Once again God's humor showed in the life of Madge.

Verse 15 says, "She gets up before dawn to prepare breakfast for her household and plan the day's work for her servant girls" (NLT). Ladies, our friend Madge had *servants*! No wonder she could rise before dawn, make her own bed linens, plant vineyards, and sell her goods to merchants. No wonder she could laugh at the days to come! I think we all could laugh more if someone else was scrubbing our floors, cleaning our toilets, and cooking our food.

I hope you know I'm saying all of this in jest. As moms, we should view the Proverbs 31 woman as a godly example. Her template for life should help us grow, learn, and gain new skills. However, perfection is *not* part of the equation. Seeking to be women after God's own heart is the goal. We simply need to be the moms God created us to be.

While I wasn't the most organized, talented, or patient mom on the planet, I passed on as many good qualities to my children as I could, but I wasn't perfect. My son, who is now thirty-two, is an amazing worship pastor and is studying to become a lead pastor. All along, God knew he needed a creative mom to help inspire him toward ministry. (Plus, he was the only guy on his college floor who knew how to do laundry. Cha-ching! Mom win!) My daughter however, took after her dad. The two of them have always been tasked with keeping my son and me focused when we become distracted. (Plus, they are both hilarious and bring tons of laughter to our family unit!) The bottom line is we need each other to balance our shortcomings and encourage our strengths.

Over the years, I've learned to respond instead of react. As I matured (code word for "getting old"), my instant Old-Yeller reactions improved significantly. In the footsteps of Madge, our Proverbs 31 woman, I've learned how to "laugh at the days to come" (v. 25 NIV). I have tried to stop taking things so seriously and go with the ebb and flow of motherhood.

The book of Philippians is probably my favorite book of the Bible. In it Paul wrote, "Being confident of this, that He who began a good work in you will carry it on to completion until the day of Christ Jesus" (PHILIPPIANS 1:6 NIV). I love how THE MESSAGE communicates this: "There has never been the slightest doubt in my mind that the God who started this great work in you would keep at it and bring it to a flourishing finish on the very day Christ Jesus appears."

Sister, He who began a good work in you will complete it, which means He will *keep at it* and bring you to a flourishing finish. Isn't that a beautiful picture of Christ working in you?

He doesn't give up on you. He loves you and created you to be who *He* wants and needs you to be. He will continue maturing and growing you until He returns.

So keep at it, momma! If God is confident in what He is doing in you and will not stop working in you, then you had better not give up on yourself. Be confident. Stop comparing. And try your best to keep that cackling green lady in check. Oh, and keep praying for that housekeeper and cook.

—MARY BETH BRADSHAW, VENICE, FLORIDA

It's That Simple

"I can't always see the perfect plan He has for my life, and I struggle at times to trust Him."

It was a beautiful Saturday afternoon in July. After working a twelve-hour night shift, I rose from a peaceful four-hour slumber. Gathering myself together, I walked up the hallway toward the animated sounds of my husband, two children, and Cartoon Network blaring in the background. I greeted everyone and made a beeline to the kitchen for an early afternoon cup of coffee, which I desperately needed in order to form complete sentences and thoughts.

My four-year-old daughter, Lalah, soon joined me in the kitchen. While I waited for the caffeine to kick in, she talked about what she, her brother, and her dad had done for entertainment the previous night. Hearing my kids' nighttime adventures with Dad is typically a source of laughter. As King Solomon says in Ecclesiastes 3:4: "A time to weep, and a time to laugh; a time to mourn, and a time to dance" (ESV). Some of these nighttime stories elicit all the above!

Lalah told me they watched the movie *Babe* and ate popcorn. My seven-year-old son, Vincent, yelled from the living room that another goldfish had jumped out of the aquarium onto the carpet. He described some distinct characteristics of his appearance, like missing sections in his fins. Sighing heavily, I thought to myself how I keep telling my husband that we need to get rid of that shark fish! *He is terrorizing the other inhabitants of our increasingly shrinking fifty-foot aquatic ecosystem.* I secretly pondered how I could sneak the shark fish out of the tank without anyone noticing his lurking presence is absent.

My preschooler continued talking. "Mom, can we get a 'cuzzi in the backyard?" she asked.

Tilting my head in confusion, I asked her, "Can we get a what?"

She answered, "You remember, like when we went to Myrtle Beach and stayed in the hotel? You and dad got in the 'cu-zzi?" She was sure to emphasize each syllable of *'cuzzi* so I could understand what she was clearly mispronouncing.

I laughed without spilling any of my precious coffee. Ah, a Jacuzzi! I corrected her pronunciation. "A Jacuzzi, Lalah. And no, we cannot have a Jacuzzi!"

Continuing to plead her case she questioned, "But why can't we have one, Mom? Please, please, *please?*"

I firmly responded, "We just bought a new Slip 'N Slide at the beginning of the summer. I am not buying anything else!" I told her we do not need a Jacuzzi and they are expensive.

She quipped, "No, it's not, Mom! The commercial says it's toll-free!"

Well, that explained it. She had all the answers. I needed a second cup of coffee for mental clarity because she had obviously come to the table with all her facts in order. Game on!

As I got up to pour myself a refill, I collected my thoughts about this exchange. I wasn't quite sure how to approach this situation and win. Everyone who knows my daughter knows that she is persistent. I secretly wished I had an ounce of her persistence.

"Lalah, 'toll-free' does not mean that the Jacuzzi is free. The man in the commercial is saying you can call him and he will not charge you for the phone call. They will even send you a free book about the Jacuzzi and everything it can do for you, but the actual Jacuzzi costs money."

"But, Mom, he said call *toll-free* for your Jacuzzi." Lalah's hands flew up in the air as she stressed *toll-free* this time.

Oh, sweet child of mine—if only it were that simple. At that moment, I saw how innocently she accepted and trusted words freely. She had heard this stranger on the TV yelling, "Call toll-free now!" She believed what he said, not completely understanding, and thought she could receive it because he said it.

Do we as Christians accept and trust the Word of God freely? Jesus said, "It is written: 'Man shall not live on bread alone, but on every word that comes from the mouth of God'" (MATTHEW 4:4 NIV). Do I trust *every* word in the Bible? *Everything* God shares with me in prayer? I know Him as my Father—He wouldn't steer me wrong! When God speaks to me, do I accept what He says? Or do I try to figure out if He really meant something else? Do I trust that He can deliver *every* promise that He has made? I can't always see the perfect plan He has for my life, and I struggle at times to trust Him.

I got a lesson about acceptance and trust from my discussion with my baby girl on that beautiful day. After another twenty minutes of attempting to explain that only the call and the brochure cost nothing, Lalah still did not understand. Nor did she convince me to get a Jacuzzi. She did, however, accept and trust my explanation over whatever Mr. Cuzzi said. She trusted me because of our relationship. She relies on me and my husband. Even though she may not fully understand what is going on, I have shown as her mother that I am consistent, predictable, and reliable. She can trust my word.

"Trust in the Lord with all your heart and lean not on your own understanding; in all your ways submit to Him, and He will make your paths straight" (Proverbs 3:5–6 niv). I try hard to live out the words in these verses. My prayer is that we become totally dependent on God as little children depend on their parents. He has already shown and keeps showing Himself to be consistent, predictable, and reliable in our lives. Because of our relationship with our Father, we can trust and believe *whatever* He says! It's just that simple.

—LABRITA DENNING, CIBOLO, TEXAS

Open Arms

*"And then it hit me, not like a lightning bolt
but maybe a slow, dull thump—
Jesus doesn't roll His eyes at us."*

My daughter, Charlie, is three years old, sweet, spunky, and kind. She has rosy cheeks and the biggest blue eyes you have ever seen. When she was born, she was one of those bald babies that everyone assumed was a boy, until her second birthday when she sported the cutest and wildest blonde curls that framed her darling face. I know every mom says their kids are the cutest (and rightfully so) and I'm no exception. Charlie is our spunky little girl who is the most wonderful kid in the world.

Now, I'll be honest. Our daughter is generally obedient but also generally three years old. And there are some things God built into three-year-olds that baffle and perplex their parents—things like the constant question of *why*, the pushback, and the testing of boundaries. These are normal three-year-old behaviors, but they're still exhausting to say the least!

Charlie loves to mix paint and bring sticks into the house. She simultaneously adores and pesters her baby sister, Ginny. She dances uninhibitedly, but she is shy when a stranger walks by and says hello. She goes through the whole bedtime process, the sweet kisses, and the singing of "Jesus Loves Me," only to wait until the door has been closed to yell, "Mom! I don't want to go to sleep!" We sigh and pretend we can't hear her, crossing our fingers that she'll give up before she wakes her baby sister.

As we experienced sheltering in place due to the world-changing COVID-19 pandemic, Charlie didn't go to her preschool two days a week. She didn't get to see her grandparents or be babysat by her two favorite high school girls. She missed going to the library with her great-grandpa and her younger cousin on Wednesdays. She missed going to the grocery store with me and riding on her daddy's shoulders through Costco. She *really* missed playing at the park and having her friends over for playdates.

Along with all that, Charlie wasn't much of a fan of church at home. While she didn't mind sitting together and worshiping, as soon as our pastor started preaching, she began her weekly distraction and attention-getting techniques. She climbed into our laps and asked us to read her books. She wrestled with and rolled on top of her seven-month-old sister. She danced in front of the TV and tried to pull us up to join her in dancing. We did our best to bring her close, include her, or distract her with her own things to do. But mostly we tried to ignore her and listen to the pastor.

A few weeks into this Sunday morning attention-getting routine, I found myself annoyed from the start, just wanting to enjoy the sermon without distraction. I tried to ignore what Charlie was doing and hardly noticed that she was climbing on our dog, Indie. Then, out of the corner of my eye, I saw our sweet, gentle dog finally stand up and walk away from said child climbing on her. This promptly caused Charlie to fall forward and hit her face on the floor. She came up screaming and crying. She had hit her lip.

I didn't respond well. I just sighed and rolled my eyes. She looked at me through tear-blurred eyes, and I shrugged and shook my head, eyebrows raised in judgment. I was holding little Ginny—my excuse to do nothing. I didn't lean close or rush to hug her. So she looked to her dad through the tears. "What happened?" he asked.

I rolled my eyes. "She was climbing on the dog—again. I tell her *every single day* not to climb on Indie. This happens every time."

He picked up Charlie and sat her on his lap. She cried for a little while, but the person she wanted was me, and I didn't want to give her comfort. I wanted her to know that what she did was wrong. And her hurt lip was the result of the decision she made. After a minute, she crawled over to me and put her head in my lap. I patted her back somewhat reluctantly. If I comforted her, she might think her behavior was okay. So I only offered a little. I patted her back and said, "I'm sorry you hurt your lip. I guess you shouldn't have been climbing on Indie."

Our morning moved on. Charlie sat in her daddy's lap a few more minutes and then started playing with her dollhouse. We finished our church service and prepared for lunch. Later in the day, I took a walk and found myself thinking about some of my hang-ups. And then it hit me, not like a lightning bolt but maybe a slow, dull thump—Jesus doesn't roll His eyes at us.

Jesus is kind. There is never any hesitation to His open arms. When I am hurt and upset, crying out for love and compassion, He is there. He is present. He is waiting and longing for me to run to Him. When I make a choice that I know is wrong, that I have made a thousand times and I know will get me into trouble, I end up with a busted lip, running and crying to Him—again. But instead of giving me the cold shoulder, He is ready, not with an "I told you so" or even a hesitant pat on the back but with His nothing-held-back kind of love.

I'm reminded of I John 1:9: "If we confess our sins, he is faithful and just to forgive us our sins and to cleanse us from all unrighteousness" (ESV). This verse doesn't say Jesus will only forgive us after we've learned our lesson. It says, "If we confess our sins, he is faithful and just to forgive."

Jesus doesn't have our hang-ups. He knows when we've learned our lessons. He doesn't have to say "I told you so" before giving us comfort. He holds us and says, "I know, I know. I love you." The consequences we receive are enough. This world lets us know when we've done wrong. Jesus doesn't shelter us from those consequences. However, each and every time we fall, He is kind.

I want to be kind like Jesus. I want to let my children make their own choices, and I want to love them unconditionally—ready with arms open. I want them to feel, see, and know that their mother is doing her best to be like Jesus. And most of all, I want my children to know they are allowed to make mistakes and still be loved and welcomed with open arms.

—ALICEN HUGHES, SAN LUIS OBISPO, CALIFORNIA

Blended Life

*"God wasn't going to relent,
because He wanted to show me a new perspective
on our situation. He reminded me that
our kids had wanted us to get married.
Deep down, they desired a happy family."*

Several years ago, I was on a quest for healthy eating, and a friend of mine recommended I make a breakfast smoothie to start the day. She said, "Just throw fruits and vegetables into a blender, add ice and a little sweetener, and you'll have yourself a yummy smoothie!" I choked a smoothie down and quickly realized there are some ingredients that do *not* go together—no matter how much sweetener you add!

Little did I know how that smoothie incident would play a symbolic role in my life, as I took the plunge into marriage for the second time and formed a blended family with my new husband, Trey. Even though our wedding day was like a fairy tale, and all five of our children were involved in the ceremony, I mistakenly believed we could combine all kinds of personalities into one big, happy family as long as we sprinkled the mix with lots of love. Boy, was I wrong.

I'd diligently researched blended family dynamics, and all the resources had said, "This will be the hardest thing you have ever done." Every article I read said to expect anger and resentment from the children. The books warned that Trey and I were choosing the worst possible time in our kids' lives to get married—the adolescent years. And honestly, the daunting statistics of failure were stark. Yet, even as I read all those dire warnings, I said to myself, "It won't be like that for us." After all, we went to premarital counseling. We prayed together every day. And I was a counselor myself! I was convinced we would *not* be one of those statistics.

But despite all our planning, praying, and hoping for the best, the blending of our families did not go well. My oldest stepdaughter and my youngest son were particularly resistant. Our nights often turned into arguments. Trey and his daughter had frequent conflicts too. And by the time we reached our first wedding anniversary, I questioned my decision to marry again. The more the kids resisted, the harder I worked to "add sweetener" to our blended family. Resentment continued to build, and most nights I retreated to our closet and comforted myself with Doritos and chocolate. (Oh, and did I mention I cried a lot?)

In the first three years of our marriage, we had so many terrible events happen, I began to dread what would come next. My younger son began to skip school and do drugs. One night, he and I had a heated argument over a video game and I hurled his Xbox into the wall—not one of my finer moments. He ended up pushing me, and my husband had to restrain him. He was so angry, he left our home and lived with my ex-husband for several months.

The relationship between my oldest stepdaughter and her dad disintegrated. One night she snuck out and refused to come home. She often told him hurtful things like, "I don't want a relationship with you." On top of all that, another devastating ingredient was added to the blender: my husband's ex-wife engaged us in a child support battle that drained us both financially and emotionally.

Through all of this, I continued my morning devotions, but they felt hollow and empty. One morning, Romans 8:28 appeared in my study, and I literally rolled my eyes because I didn't want to read it. That particular verse had been the theme verse for our marriage and family. It was a promise God had given us when we were dating. Even though I *really* didn't want to read it that day, I forced myself to push through.

"And we know that God causes everything to work together for the good of those who love God and are called according to His purpose for them" (NLT).

As I concentrated on the words and let them soak into my parched, weary heart, I realized that nothing about our blended family seemed "good." I read the verse again but felt despair instead of hope.

Later that day, I had an unexpected encounter with God as I was sitting in the closet with Doritos and chocolate— again. I was venting to Him about our situation, and He stopped me in my tracks. It was one of those times when God wasn't going to relent, because He wanted to show me a new perspective on our situation. He reminded me that our kids had wanted us to get married. Deep down, they desired a happy family. Our blended family was good, but it also represented loss to the kids. After all, they'd experienced major life changes. And any time we experience life changes, even if they're good, a type of grieving process occurs. Our kids didn't know how to verbalize or process their grief, so it materialized as anger and bad behavior.

At that moment, in my "venting" closet, I put down the Doritos and chocolate. For the first time, I began to see the situation from their vantage point. Then, God gave me clear direction. "You need to repent to your children." Romans

8:28 played over and over in my mind, and I felt a little hope. Could God bring good to our situation after all?

Shortly after, I took my oldest stepdaughter to lunch. I apologized for my lack of understanding. It was a terrifying, vulnerable moment. She looked at me in a way she never had before. Her eyes filled with tears, and it was as if I finally saw her heart for the first time. She accepted my apology and thanked me. It was a turning point in our relationship.

I treated my younger son to dinner and apologized for not being more compassionate about his grief. He had the same reaction. He thanked me and hugged me. My oldest son, who I thought was the most accepting of the transition, had the same feelings as the other two kids. Again, I apologized. And guess what? I got the same reaction of forgiveness.

Today, almost five years later, it is still hard! Our marriage and blended family take diligent work. Every. Single. Day. I continue to sprinkle love and sweetener, but the biggest ingredient I add is a willingness to apologize when I mess up. It's a vulnerable position, but it has created an environment where our kids feel like they are allowed to mess up too.

The other day, my youngest stepdaughter made a smoothie. Scenes from the last five years scrolled through my mind. Some made me shudder and some made me sad, but some made me smile. Again, I thought of Romans 8:28 and realized that even though some ingredients in our blended family were not so good, I could count on the promises of God. I also realized that I don't like smoothies for breakfast—give me Doritos and chocolate any day!

—ANGIE FOUTS-HYATT, PARKER, COLORADO

Stained Glass Life

*"I deeply resonate with those stained glass images,
purposefully shattered and remade
into one of His works of art."*

My background is in science, but I have an artist's soul. I love art and have always gravitated to great painters of the Renaissance. The crisp lines and intricate details appeal to my need for order, while the rich color and layered meanings captivate my imagination. Abstract works, however, elicit a completely different reaction in me. While my grade school son can talk at length about texture, mood, and contrast, when it comes to abstract modern art, I'm usually lost. The pieces often feel disjointed and off-kilter to me. In order for me to enjoy abstract art, I find that I must change my perspective and rearrange my ideas to fit the art, not make the art fit me. And for some reason, it's uncomfortable.

However, I have the nagging feeling that Jesus is more like my son. I imagine He loves the mixed-media, nonsensical creations that might feel unworthy of attention at first glance. Perhaps the artists of old weren't that far off when they decorated the ancient cathedrals with mix-and-match stained glass. After all, those beautifully broken pieces, separated by dark lines and thrown together to form an image, allow the greater art of the sun to shine through.

Comparing this to the beautiful chaos of motherhood— this sanctified season of survival—I can't help but notice tiny miracles amid the mundane. There's a masterpiece being created in my own motherhood journey. And while I'm still adjusting to some of the bold strokes and jarring additions—often feeling broken in the process—I deeply resonate with those stained glass images, purposefully shattered and remade into one of His works of art.

Recently, I was thumbing through one of my past journals and read the opening of this sad paragraph dated April 27, 2013:

> I ended my African-adventure journal yesterday and picked up this American-hospital journal today. As I recall the ups and downs and the miracles that were going to happen during our years in Africa, I feel like most of our hopes and dreams were lost long ago. We've fought hard just to maintain our hold on Christ, this last year in particular. It seems like it's been a very long time since we've thrived.

Five months before I wrote this, I'd given birth to a very broken little baby. He was my third child—my second son. He came into this world like no baby should, desperately sick and fighting for his life. I remember waking up in an African hospital and being told by the doctor that if I wanted to see my baby alive, I needed to come to the tiny NICU they'd set up. I had no idea it was the first day of a five-month NICU stay that ultimately ended in our medical evacuation to the States. I had no idea it was the end of our African dreams.

Today, I'm writing to all the mothers walking out a different dream for motherhood. Maybe, like me, your hopes and dreams feel a little shattered, a little broken. Maybe your world includes more doctor's appointments than you expected. Maybe your prayers seem to go unanswered. There are so many variations to the complexities of parenting! Only you know your story, and only you know the dreams that have slipped away as your reality unfolds.

Sometimes I find myself standing next to my son's bed. He's seven years old now and shares a room with his big brother. But instead of a little-boy race car bed, he sleeps in a hospital bed. His older brother happily sets army men around his wheelchair, and my toddler climbs into his bed to play with his sensory toys. His big sister sings him songs to calm him down, and honestly, there are days when these scenes break my heart.

Grady will never be the child we'd hoped for—to make our numbers "even" on roller coaster rides. He'll never run free on the wild continent that saw his first breath. But he is here. And, oh, how he loves his mama! His hugs are magical, and he runs his hands through my hair for hours while I rest my head on his chair. My son, who was so broken, is now a ray of sunshine and love. The physical care can be exhausting, but his sweet giggles and contagious laugh permeate our home.

Over the years, I've released my dreams for my motherhood like a bunch of balloons. Not in one mighty relinquishing but one by one in a slow, brave offering to the Creator of all good things. And I'll probably keep releasing them as the years go on, for nothing is static on this journey.

But here's the beauty: We are entrusting our hopes, visions, and dreams to an Artist, not to the vast expanse of the universe. He asks us to trust Him with all those half-whispered ideas of how motherhood should look. Then, He takes us deeper and asks us to give Him the shattered remnants when those dreams fall to pieces. The Artist takes our brokenness and breathes new life into us.

Ecclesiastes 3:11 says, "He has made everything beautiful in its time" (NIV). This verse is a confirmation of our Master Artist who is waiting to gather our broken pieces and form a masterpiece. As we adjust our hearts to see His hands working out our motherhood journeys, we begin to see things as the Creator sees them. We can stand back and look at our stained glass lives and see His light shining through. And as we adjust our eyes to see the illogical beauty, we can let that rainbow of warmth comfort our hearts today. After all, He is still creating your motherhood story, and it is truly a work of art.

—EJ RODGERS, KAHALU'U, HAWAII

Digging Holes

*"I often feel like my days equate to digging a hole,
filling it up again, and repeating the sequence
of events over and over."*

Last summer, my seven-year-old triplet boys decided to dig a hole in the front yard. They made a unified decision that a patch of earth where the grass had not grown was the perfect place to dig a tunnel.

At the beginning of their massive undertaking, one son informed me that I would need to purchase each of them a miner's helmet—the kind with a light on top. After all, how could they explore an underground tunnel with no light? He assured me that safety was of utmost importance to them, and that no matter how far into the earth he traveled, he would always come home to me. Then, the boys marched into the garage and begged their dad for digging utensils. He offered them shovels, but they decided that shovels would not do. Each boy picked a man-sized hammer, and off they trudged to dig their hole to reach the center of the earth.

For weeks, I watched them work on that hole. I peeked at them from the front window while I vacuumed the floor. I curiously eyed them as I worked from the front porch. They pounded that North Carolina clay tirelessly with the claw side of the hammer, each boy taking turns in order to maximize their digging potential. On a particularly hot day at the beginning of July, one of my sons decided it would be great fun to bury a tennis ball. His brother suggested that the hole was the perfect place to bury it. The boys placed the yellow ball in the hole, then scooped the mounds of freshly dug dirt over it. However, almost immediately afterward, one brother realized their grave error. The hole they had so diligently worked on all summer had disappeared! Once again, they picked up their hammers and began digging their tunnel. This scenario played out all summer long. They worked feverishly on digging their hole, only to cover it up for various reasons. By the time school began in August, the patch of earth looked exactly as it did at the very beginning of summer.

Oh, how motherhood can sometimes feel like that digging project! For me, as a mom of four elementary-aged kids, I often feel like my days equate to digging a hole, filling it up again, and repeating the sequence of events over and over. I vacuum the floors, only to have them dirtied in minutes. I wash the dishes, only to find the sink filled once again. I lose count of how many loads of laundry I wash each week. Motherhood with young children can feel like a string of ordinary days bound together with crumbs and sand. The end of the month arrives, and it seems like I am right back where I started—with nothing to show for my efforts.

Whenever I feel like I've lost joy in the journey, I like to read the familiar story of Mary and Martha. The passage in Luke 10, though short, helps me overcome the despondency that accompanies my never-ending to-do list:

As Jesus and the disciples continued on their way to Jerusalem, they came to a certain village where a woman named Martha welcomed Him into her home. Her sister, Mary, sat at the Lord's feet, listening to what He taught. But Martha was distracted by the big dinner she was preparing. She came to Jesus and said, "Lord, doesn't it seem unfair to you that my sister just sits here while I do all the work? Tell her to come and help me."

But the Lord said to her, "My dear Martha, you are worried and upset over all these details! There is only one thing worth being concerned about. Mary has discovered it, and it will not be taken away from her." (vv. 38–42 NLT)

I wish I could say that I am most like Mary in this story. I picture her in my head, so enthralled with the experience of being near Jesus that other tasks are completely forgotten. Unfortunately, I am much more like Martha. If Martha and I could sit down and have a chat, I believe she would tell me all about her good intentions. Because Jesus was in her home, I imagine she would tell me how she wanted every detail of the dinner to be flawless for Him. Yet in the process of the tasks, she lost the joy in what she was preparing and the joy of being in His presence.

I don't know about you, but I have a mental image of what sort of mother that I want to be. However, the picturesque mother in my mind is not always a reflection of a biblical mother. Rather, it's a confusing compilation of what others have made me feel like I *should* be. Too much Pinterest and not enough Jesus always makes me feel like an inadequate mother! And it's in those moments that I find myself focusing on the aspects of motherhood that I *have* to do rather than those that I *get* to do. I have to clean sand off the floor—again. I have to cook dinner—again. I have to help them with homework—again.

But even as I struggle, I find that the more that I view my daily tasks in light of the Mary and Martha story, the more my days seem less like digging an unending hole and more like the joyful journey God intended it to be. I'm not sure that I will ever be completely like Mary in the Bible story, but I sure am willing to try! Will you join me in this process? I encourage you to revisit the familiar story and put some of the joy back into your motherhood journey. And while you're at it, don't forget to bring a few other "Martha" moms along with you!

—MELANIE EAST, WALNUT COVE, NORTH CAROLINA

Playtime Wins

*"In the serious and silly moments,
our Creator chooses to be present with His kids.
In all situations, He chooses to make Himself known."*

When I think back to the effects of the COVID-19 pandemic on our home, several choice words come to mind: *different, loud,* and *messy beyond belief.* At first, I tried to keep up with the majority of the housework, but that was quickly thrown out the window—literally. My three wild boys seem to think throwing toys out the bedroom window is a hilarious form of entertainment. Thank God for His grace and humor!

In such an unknown time, it was hard to establish routines or keep anything normal. My boys missed regular activities like going to school, playing in parks, and being with their friends. It seemed like so much had been taken away, and it was easy for us to focus on what we were lacking. But God also made room for unexpected blessings like creativity, flexibility, and play. And when it comes to play, no one plays harder than our middle son, Nathan.

Nate is only five, but soon after he was born, we got a taste of who he was made to be. He is our strong little warrior. He loves fiercely and fights for those he treasures. We often call him our "spicy meatball" because there's a fire burning inside of him, and his emotions rise quickly to the surface—especially if he is passionate about something. During the pandemic lockdown, Nate made it his goal to spend extensive amounts of time playing his favorite battle game with Mama called Beat the Beast. It didn't matter what an object was, it could and would be transformed into a bad guy. A stuffed animal, a spatula, Lego blocks—everything was a villain that must be defeated.

Together, we moved from one level to the next, going from room to room, to destroy all evil (until Mommy said she had to make lunch or take a bathroom break). Sometimes I found myself scanning the home for pressing tasks that needed to get done, while simultaneously trying to remain present with my son. (For the record, I'm a horrible multitasker.) Almost immediately, tension started forming in my heart and my mind became distracted. "Mom, pay attention! The beast is coming!" I would hear. That's when I would jolt out of multitask mode and quickly refocus on my boy. But still, in the back of my mind I wondered. . .

> Is this what I am supposed to be doing right now?
> Is playing with my kids more important than the laundry piled on the floor?
> How is God present in these moments of play?
> Why do I feel guilty for not being able to do it all?

One night, I was putting the boys to bed after playing round 5,062 of Beat the Beast. As I covered Nathan with his blanket, his vibrant eyes got wide and he asked, "Mom, did you know Jesus beats the bad guys, too?"

I stopped what I was doing and smiled. "That's right, babe! And He wins every single time."

I knew my son's comment was a gift from God. The Lord heard the busy cycle of thoughts in my mind and understood I was in desperate need of encouragement. He knew my warrior baby's words would show me what my soul really needed. Because God is always with us, He reveals Himself in everything we do. In the serious and silly moments, our Creator chooses to be present with His kids. In all situations, He chooses to make Himself known.

Play has a plethora of purposes. It helps us connect with our children and reassures them of their worth. It shows them we value their interests and persuades them of our care. But it goes even further. Playtime gives us the divine opportunity to play out what is true. Through games and imagination, we have the privilege of bringing eternal realities to light. The Bible comes alive in the stories we play.

I have not been able to look at "Beat the Beast" the same way since that sweet conversation with Nate. In the middle of a make-believe game, the Lord showed me that He is the reigning King and all His sons and daughters have won. Through every battle, through each of our struggles, Christ has given us the power to overcome. The enemy tries to throw us off course. He tries to trip us up. But the gospel has already paved the way to victory, and God's grace covers it all.

We are raising little warriors who will one day change the world. They will go after their enemy and tear apart his plans. They will bring the message of hope and fight for what is true. It's important for us to remember God is always moving in our families. He uses everything to develop us, strengthen us, and reveal more about His love. Nothing is ever wasted. No time invested will return void. We are making such a difference. We are leading their hearts well.

Psalm 127:4–5 says, "Like arrows in the hand of a warrior are the children of one's youth. Blessed is the man who fills his quiver with them!" (ESV).

Our little warriors are the biggest blessings in our quivers. And choosing time with them over week-old laundry is a good thing. The laundry will still be there when we've exhausted our Beat-the-Beast skills. If I could give you any encouragement during this season of parenting, it would be this: Keep going, Mama. Keep loving, keep playing, keep growing. Keep allowing God to show up daily in your life. Let Him be creative in the ways He makes Himself known. Don't let the enemy make you doubt who you're called to be or what you're called to do. That battle has been won, and the beast has been beaten. You can stand tall in Christ because His victory will help you walk out every inch of motherhood and life.

—BECKY BERESFORD, HUNTLEY, ILLINOIS

This Is the Way

*"Once I began to think about how much
I loved my daughter, I began to better understand
God's heart for me."*

It was the fifth time I had circled the old town square looking for a parking spot. I had never had trouble before finding a place to park in front of the downtown building where my children took their weekly music lessons. I thought we had left in enough time to arrive at least five minutes early, but we had been driving around the block for what felt like an eternity. To make matters worse, not only did I have to get my daughter to her violin lesson in just a couple of minutes, but I also had my five other children (one who was an infant), a cello, two violins, a diaper bag, and three backpacks that needed to get inside as well. With each passing minute, my anxiety level grew. Adding to my frustration, a light rain had begun to dampen the windshield, and I didn't have an umbrella. *Now we are going to be late and wet,* I thought to myself. *I wish I was the mom who had it all together. Why can't I do better? Why do I never allow enough time?*

Fortunately, after one more circle around the block, a car finally backed out of its spot and I pulled our large van in quickly. As I put the van in park, I began to give everyone their marching orders: "Emma, grab your violin and your backpack and then start walking to your lesson. Davis, grab your backpack and cello and wait for me on the sidewalk.

Daniel, stand on the sidewalk and hold your sisters' hands." I gathered the rest of our belongings from the rear of our van as quickly as I could. Then I slipped the diaper bag on my shoulder, took my son from his car seat, and headed toward the studio. We had parked a full block farther away than usual, but hopefully we would only be a minute or two late and only slightly wet if we hurried.

As I watched my daughter walk swiftly down the street ahead of us, I reflected on how proud I was of her confidence and independence. Being the oldest of six, she was a natural leader and very dependable. She was also good at following directions, and at times like this, I was very thankful for her maturity.

Just at that moment, my daughter, about a half block ahead of us, came upon an intersection and suddenly disappeared from my view. I thought she knew that we needed to go straight to reach the music studio; however, since we were in such a hurry and had parked farther away than usual, she had gotten disoriented and turned left a block before our destination. *Where is she going?* I thought to myself. Beginning to panic slightly, I picked up my pace the best I could while carrying my little ones and all their belongings. I didn't want Emma to get any farther out of my sight. As I came upon the intersection, I looked to see Emma now swiftly walking down a side road in a completely wrong direction!

In a full panic, I began to call her name, but she couldn't hear me and just kept walking. I could not catch up to her, so I yelled out even louder, "Emma, Emma, come back! You're going the wrong way!" Thankfully, as soon as she heard me calling her name, she stopped. Quickly she turned around and ran back toward me grinning. As she got closer to me she called out, "Sorry, Mom, I must have gotten confused and turned around." When she was safely by my side, I gave her the correct directions. With a smile on her face and a bounce in her step, she headed off once again, this time going in the right direction.

A few months later, I was having a diffcult time making a crucial decision that would affect the future of our family. I pondered the options over and over in my head. Each choice seemed to have its own set of pros and cons. The longer my indecision lasted, the more I became paralyzed by the fear of making the wrong choice. I thought, *What if I make the wrong decision and then God can't work? What if I do something that isn't God's will? What if I mess everything up? What if...?*

God sweetly brought to my remembrance the day my daughter had confidently headed in the wrong direction. As I thought about my daughter, I also reflected on my attitude toward her.

Even when she accidentally went down the wrong street, her heart clearly wanted to honor and obey me. When she heard me calling her name, she immediately responded to my voice. She was constantly listening for me. I wasn't mad at her for going the wrong way. In fact, I delighted in her confidence and bravery. I was glad to see her quickly come back and listen again for the directions.

Once I began to think about how much I loved my daughter, I began to better understand God's heart for me.

With the decision still weighing heavy on my heart, I knew that God loved my family and me and wanted me to make the right decision. I knew I could trust Him to help me make a wise decision, and I could also trust Him to call my name and lead me back if I got something wrong.

Isaiah 30:21 has always been a favorite Scripture of mine, especially when I don't know which way to go. It says, "Whether you turn to the right or to the left, your ears will hear a voice behind you, saying, 'This is the way; walk in it'" (NIV). I love that this verse points to a voice leading from behind, not out in front! We must first listen, then step out in faith and keep listening for His voice to guide us.

Like my daughter, sometimes we will get it wrong. Thankfully we have a loving heavenly Father who corrects and guides us each step along the way. It is His perfect love that casts out all fear, even the fear of making the wrong decision!

—KIM BORDERS, CLARKSVILLE, TENNESSEE

When Reality Rules

"Keep in mind that good things never happen overnight, so understand your purpose and stick with it."

Reality is a messy mesh of scenarios and so is motherhood. Even though I'm well past the young children stage, with grown kids who've given me ten grandchildren, I still remember the earlier years.

I recall the days of scrubbing the floor, cleaning the house, and making sure everything looked perfect. I tried so hard to make sure the beds were made without a wrinkle. Sparkling bathrooms, with the smell of pine seeping down the halls, colliding with the aroma of chocolate chip cookies baking in the oven, made me feel like everything was right in the world.

I spent many mornings working hard so I could enjoy a mug of fresh coffee and a great book, as soft music played in the background. What a life! To me, those moments almost mirrored what heaven would be like. Then, out of nowhere, sudden terror would hit my perfect, heavenly home. The youngest kids would wake up from nap time. The bigger kids would arrive home from school. And suddenly the scene would turn from heavenly bliss to, well, *reality*.

One afternoon, my neatly scrubbed floor was "accidentally" covered with an entire pitcher of grape juice. At that moment, my "mighty mom" visions of strength and wisdom quickly vanished into a sudden dose of sticky reality. With the guilty child completely drenched in grape juice— the permanent, purple kind, mind you—and the inside of the refrigerator flooded, the other kids perceived it to be the perfect time to help clean up. Of course, right in the middle of the chaos, the doorbell rang.

The plumber, whom I'd called two weeks earlier, had arrived to fix the dishwasher. Wonderful! With sticky grape juice on the floor, it was the perfect time for him to trample through the entry way. And his odor? It could've drowned out the pine, freshly baked cookies, *and* potpourri smell all at once!

After *finally* getting the kitchen cleaned, I moved into the family room where my wonderful blessings from God had Lincoln Logs, Legos, and video tapes (now replaced by DVDs) strung all over the floor. Cushions were off the couch and being used as a trampoline. Moving on to the bedrooms, the once wrinkle-free beds were being used as torpedo destinations with flying leaps from the end of the hallway.

How often my beautiful world was turned from bliss to wretchedness. My joyful attitude would instantly resort to full, carnal anger. And I found myself wondering how, in such a short amount of time, could something so beautiful turn so horrid? That's when I'd be forced back into reality. Because reality rules in this great big world.

Perfection in motherhood is not the goal. Whether it's "keeping up with the Joneses," as we used to say, or simply not caring because you're so exhausted, motherhood is less about being perfect and more about being present.

Moms, I get it. The daily grind of being a mother of children, with diapers, unending laundry, kids in and out, and various projects, is a constant job of putting out fires. It's a never-ending flurry of activity and chaos. You order the kids outside, then order them back in. You tell them to turn off the TV, then turn it back on again for a moment of peace. It's an ongoing barrage of activity! And it puts us in the difficult place of finding balance and harmony on a constant roller coaster ride.

During those days, I played the image game many times, trying to keep that perfect facade. Other times, I just gave up and didn't care how messy everything got. Either way, neither scenario played out well. So if reality rules, how do we find the balance? How do we keep ourselves present without going crazy in the chaos? I have a few thoughts from my thirty-six years of being a momma that might help you move from one day to the next.

Pursue purpose, not perfection

No one is expecting you to be perfect. That notion comes from competing with those around you. Social media portrays Disney-like birthday parties and perfect family pictures. And it looks so effortless! But if we're really honest, we know there is more behind the scenes. Building our children into great adults has nothing to do with a perfect picture. We spend countless days training and molding them, teaching them how to make the right choices, perceive life, and respond wisely. Keep in mind that good things never happen overnight, so understand your purpose and stick with it.

Pursue time for yourself

Even if it's only half an hour before the kids get up, set that alarm, get your coffee, and sit in the silence of the early morning hours. This will help you clear your head, rest your soul, and spend time with God. Even sitting in silence will allow you to declutter your brain so you will be able to see, hear, and respond with more clarity.

Pursue balance

Balance is a daily reward. It will look different from day to day, but you will know when you've attained it. Some days you will feel like you've taken a step backward, but other days you will feel like you've accomplishment something amazing. Just know that it's the small victories that keep your heart moving forward instead of getting discouraged. With balance, your best will be best.

Pursue flexibility

Sometimes flexibility comes naturally. Other times, you have to acquire the skill. Either way, you have to learn how to bend. Rigidity breaks the spirit—yours and that of everyone around you. Learning to give a little will help you reach your goal of peace and harmony. Of course, certain absolutes need to be upheld, but most of the time you can remain flexible.

In my home, we always tried to use the phrase "help me understand." This would allow for conversations to continue rather than shut down. Accusations usually stop a discussion in its tracks, but if we can have an ear to hear what is really trying to be communicated and use the wisdom of our years to help decipher the real issue, there will be agreement (or at least compromise). It just takes a little time and flexibility, so be willing to bend.

Ecclesiastes 3:4 says there is "a time to weep, and a time to laugh; a time to mourn, and a time to dance" (NKJV). The next time reality rules and upheaval arrives, just remember that bad days are born for our good and there is a time for everything. Remember your purpose, find the balance, practice flexibility, and for goodness' sake, keep it real.

—KAREN HAGAN, MINNEAPOLIS, MINNESOTA

Rinse and Repeat

*"It's not just moms who do repetitive,
never-ending work—everyone sets up their pins
only to knock them down again."*

My childhood dream of becoming Belle, the main character from Disney's *Beauty and the Beast*, has finally come true. Each morning opens "like the one before" in my provincial home life. But instead of the captivating tales that Belle reads, my days open with a never-ending volume of Curious George. Even before breakfast is over, the story of motherhood and all its many details becomes uninteresting and mundane. Breakfast pours into block time or book time, which tumbles into modeling-dough time or coloring time. Then, there's the demand for more food with its accompanying messes and mishaps. If I'm honest, sometimes I want to give up and find my own castle (with servants included)!

On one of those mundane mornings, my boys were playing together nicely, so I seized the moment to sprint upstairs and collect the laundry to be washed. I picked up a couple of scattered shirts and unwed socks, gathered whatever was on the changing table, and tossed it all on top of the overflowing basket. I set it on my hip and weaved around blocks and plastic toy animals as I shuffled downstairs to the laundry room.

The basket landed with a *smack* on the linoleum floor, right next to another basket filled to the brim with clean clothes awaiting their return trip. There was no time to move the baskets around or make a better decision about what to do with all the clothes, as I was running late in picking up my daughter. Thankfully, my sweet boys were good sports and hopped in the car without complaint.

Later that day, I walked past the baskets and I was hit immediately with sinking regret for my previous haste, as well as my inability to remember which basket of clothes had already been washed and dried! The forensics process didn't take too long, and I managed to stuff the washing machine to the brim before being summoned away to mediate a Transformer-related dispute.

Later that afternoon, I discovered in the worst way possible that I was no Sherlock Homemaker. Even though I'd washed the correct load of laundry, I'd included something that should never, ever be washed—a pull-up diaper.

It was unused, mind you, but the mess was astronomical. Until then, I'd never realized how much liquid a diaper could hold! I pulled out the clothes, scooped the mess out of the washer, and unclogged the drain. Millions of bits of diaper filling fused to fleece pajama pants and fuzzy socks. The load would have to be rewashed after the machine was thoroughly cleaned. That day, I added my own lines to the novel *Sherlock Homemaker*: "It's elementary, Katie: be a little more selective in what items you throw into the laundry basket to be washed!"

Later that evening, after kissing tops of heads and pulling blankets up over shoulders, I sat down to read my study of Galatians. A verse popped off the page and into my heart. It was one I had read many times before, but it felt different this time. It said, "And let us not grow weary of doing good, for in due season we will reap, if we do not give up" (GALATIANS 6:9 ESV).

As a teenager reading that verse, I thought it referred to

building churches in some faraway land. But as it turns out, "doing good" can also mean doing the same chores for my family every single day.

One of my favorite Christian singers and fellow moms, Sara Groves, wrote the song "Setting Up the Pins." You may have heard it before. It's about trying to find an easy way around doing the mundane yet necessary things in life. I feel a sense of camaraderie with Sara, because I've often believed that if I just had more money or resources, I could find a way around doing the everyday things I don't always like to do. But the song also talks about finding joy in "setting up the pins" in our lives just to knock them back down again.

The reality is that it's not just moms who do repetitive, never-ending work—everyone sets up their pins only to knock them down again. Every year the earth revolves around the same sun. A seasoned teacher teaches the same lessons. The moon waxes and wanes each and every month. And doctors treat the same illnesses. Each new day begins and then ends. Even after Belle married her prince, she still lived in provincial France. She still had the same life (besides being rich and married). At the end of the day, a castle with servants doesn't make our souls any deeper or richer.

After considering the words from Sara Groves' song that God was whispering into my tired soul, I decided I would not grow weary and give up. Instead of finding a way around the mundane, or cursing it, I would thank God for it. I would thank Him for the fertile ground and the verdant little saplings that had sprung from it. I would remember the words of my wise mom who reminded me, "The work will always be there, so it's okay to sit and eat a bonbon once in a while."

In I Thessalonians 5:18, the Bible encourages, "Be thankful

in all circumstances, for this is God's will for you who belong to Christ Jesus" (NLT).

This passage reminds me to be thankful, even when I'm doing the same things over and over. I can sing while I cook—which is what Belle would do. I can dance while I wipe down counters and tables after meals. I can fold a week's worth of laundry while watching my favorite show. And little by little, I can take important steps to introduce my saplings to the necessary yet painfully routine parts of life—one rinse-and-repeat day at a time.

—KATIE TEESDALE, KNOXVILLE, TENNESSEE

Got Regret?

*"Remorse is a miserable place to dwell.
It's time to realize that God's work is progressive
and there are better days ahead."*

Have you ever looked back and thought, *Why did I do that without weighing the options and making a better decision?*

As moms, I think most of us can say we have at least one lingering regret. But here's the reality: Regret always leaves a wound that badgers our integrity. It hurts deeply. And it leaves us questioning our own discernment. Regret is painful. It stalks you during the day and wakes you up at night. It's a tagalong you wish would go away. And here's the worse part: You can't fix your mistake. You can't change it. You can't reverse it. All you can do is learn to deal with it God's way.

If your kids are old enough, you've likely experienced the wound of regret over a particular decision. One of my regrets involves my son. An eighth grader at the time, he was a fabulous athlete and had just taken up tennis. Within a year, he'd already been invited to be part of the regional league of traveling players for the summer. He was pumped!

His stepdad and I signed a contract saying he would finish the season. However, in the midst of all this teenage fame, he did what lots of teenagers do: he disobeyed the house rules and developed a defiant spirit. In his mind, he knew we had signed a contract for his summer extravaganza, so what could the consequences be?

Needless to say, I was perplexed and unsettled. I wondered whether I should let him continue to play or teach him a lesson by breaking the contract. In the end, we broke the contract. Even though I wrestled with this decision because I believe it's important to stick with commitments in life, I was hoping it would get his attention so we could focus on the problems at hand. But what followed were difficult years that I would *never* want to relive.

As cofounder of a global nonprofit outreach for single mothers, I've heard hundreds of stories of moms who wish they could redo motherhood drama. I've hurt with them, cried with them, and even envisioned biblical heroes who could join our "Regret Club." For example, remember Peter? Jesus warned Peter that he would deny Him three times. I wonder what kind of remorse Peter felt when he heard the third "cock-a-doodle-doo." And what about David's regret after he committed sin with Bathsheba while her husband was out fighting in a war? And don't forget, David's shameful actions were published for all to see—in the Bible!

Maybe, like these guys, your regret stems from a sin you committed—one you're deeply sorry about to this day. Or like me, perhaps your regret stems from sheer lack of insight, not thinking through a situation with better perception. Either way, regret is a killer! It's wedged in our brains, waiting for an opportune time to remind us all over again of our failures. So how do we as moms deal with our regrets?

While I was driving down the highway one day, God gently showed me how to soothe my regrets with the comforting acronym SELF. I quickly pulled over and jotted down my instructions: Submit, Expect, Learn, and Forgive.

If you're like me, you know that *submit* means to give up

something or to yield. But still, I found myself uncomfortably tied to my unsettling blunder. What was the secret behind the word *submit* that I didn't see? Then it came to me. I could never break free from my regret until I humbled myself under God's authority, wisdom, and power. He beckoned me by saying, "Pam, let it go and leave the outcome to Me."

But submission doesn't stand alone. It has a companion called *expectation*. What good does it do to submit under the Father's leadership but not expect Him to follow through with His word? For all of us moms who struggle with loss or missed opportunities with our kids, Romans 8:28 becomes our VBF—very best friend. In that promise, God affirms that He works all imperfections, all lapses in judgment, and all flaws together for good for those who love Him and are called according to His purpose.

Moms, this means every action yielded to Him is weaved into a higher profit. Expectation on our part is not just a wishful hope based on our own desires. It's a solid assurance based on God's character—one that is unchangeable and trustworthy. I can *expect* God to bring my regrets to a profitable end because He is faithful and just.

Through every season, there are life truths to *learn*. Until we've walked through the healing process and asked our Father, "What do You want me to learn from this?" we'll resemble a gerbil in its cage going round and round on its wheel, packing one regret upon another. But when we let God shed light on how He desires to transform our pain into possibility, we are set free from the endless cycle.

Finally, we learn to *forgive*. We let ourselves off the blame hook. After all, we were never wired to be perfect moms and win motherhood Oscars for every decision. Our moms weren't perfect, so why do we think we should be? We need to allow ourselves the freedom to do what humans do—make mistakes. If we never made mistakes, why would we need Jesus? How could He transform us into His image if we never missed the mark?

Come to think of it, regret is actually good if handled correctly. It drives us to the end of ourselves and forces us to live in a power greater than ourselves. When we *submit, expect, learn* and *forgive*, we put ourselves on the pathway to enjoy every blessing on the horizon.

I'm happy to say that my son is now grown and happily married to a wonderful wife. He is a fantastic dad to three children. Seeing him now versus when he was a teenager, I realize that remorse is a miserable place to dwell. It's time to realize that God's work is progressive and better days lie ahead. It's time to stop the fistfights with wishful do-overs. And it's time, my friends, to let regret go.

—PAM KANALY, EDMOND, OKLAHOMA

The Best Happy

*"Children need their moms—even moms
who don't feel like they have it all together."*

We adopted our sweet daughter from an orphanage in China when she was four years old. Much to our surprise, spending time together—even doing mundane things—seemed to thoroughly delight this little girl, whose early years were composed of a stark room, a handful of caregivers, and no meaningful connections.

After she'd been with us for several months, we bumped into one of her preschool buddies as we were walking through the grocery store.

"What's he doing here, Mom?" she asked.

"He and his mom are picking up some groceries," I answered.

"He has a mom?" she asked in surprise.

"Yes, of course," I told her. "All your friends at school have a mom."

She was shocked! In the orphanage, only the lucky few got a mom. And once they did, she never saw them again. It was hard for her to comprehend that in her classroom of fifteen children, each one went home to a family. At dinner that night, she shared her amazing discovery with her dad. Then, she followed it up with the statement, "I'm so happy I have a mommy and daddy!"

Often, while her older siblings were at school, she and I would take long walks together. Neighbors would see us meandering hand in hand, up and down each street in our wooded subdivision, listening to birds and noticing the wildflowers. She would look up at me with her dark brown eyes and speak her words of happiness into my heart. "I'm so happy I have a mommy and daddy!" she would repeat.

It seemed like that statement flowed so easily off her tongue. Multiple times a day, with the most serene look on her face, she would say it. Then, she would snuggle up to me and melt in my arms. What a treasure! I found her words to be such a treat, especially on days when I made mistakes or mishandled situations.

I realized that my daughter's go-to statement was a message that others needed to hear. After all, children need their moms—even moms who don't feel like they have it all together. I realized that while I certainly didn't have it all together, my daughter didn't seem to notice. She remained happy and content, just by feeling like she belonged.

Since a lot of my time is spent advocating for children who need families, I take every opportunity to show moms that perfection isn't required in order to welcome a child into their home. I even considered writing a blog titled "Never Underestimate the Value of a Mom." It was a post that needed to be written, and I planned to include a picture of my daughter's face as she smiled up at me. But, as life often goes, I got busy. The blog took a back seat while I worked with my husband to build a play set in the backyard. Then, that project gave way to planning a big birthday party for a certain little girl. And in the end, my blog post never got written.

Then, a couple of days after the big birthday party bash— and the brand-new play set—my daughter shocked me by announcing she wanted a different family. She named one of her friend's families as the one she thought would be a better fit for her! What?

But when I stopped to think about it, I realized she'd been acting out to get attention. And more importantly, I realized I hadn't heard her daily mantra in a while; I hadn't seen her smiling face looking up at me saying, "I'm so happy I have a mommy and daddy!"

Wasn't she still happy to have a mommy and daddy? What about the new swing set and fun birthday party? At first I was baffled, but the more I thought about it, the more I realized that I had gotten completely off track. I'd become so caught up in doing things *for* her, I had neglected to do things *with* her. I had focused on getting things done, and my sweet little girl had been pushed to the side.

Right around that time, I was reading my Bible and came across Proverbs 14:1: "A wise woman builds her home, but a foolish woman tears it down with her own hands" (NLT).

My mind instantly pictured a crazed woman recklessly tearing things to pieces and tossing them aside—figuratively ripping her family apart. I realized that the verse related to my situation. A wise woman builds her home by nurturing connections with those in her family, but a foolish woman gets so busy accomplishing things that she neglects what is important.

When my little girl woke up the next morning, I paused for a few minutes to rock her back and forth and look into her eyes. I told her how precious she was. Instead of scooting her out the door when it was time to go to school, we held hands while walking to the car. After school, we played in the backyard together, and that evening she helped me plant some flowers around the lamppost. Over the next several days as I became more intentional, I noticed that her attention-seeking behaviors lessened—which was a win for all of us.

Just the other day, as we were playing with dolls in her room, she stopped what she was doing and looked me straight in the eye. I saw that familiar expression on her face and knew what was coming next.

"I'm so happy I have a mommy and daddy!"

Then, as we resumed playing, my heart whispered this prayer: *Lord, may I never be so busy with my hands that I neglect the hearts of those I love.*

—KAREN M. RAPP, ANDERSON, SOUTH CAROLINA

Hands-Off Connection

"Sometimes the most loving thing is to be hands-off and become a 'guide on the side' who connects with our kids through prayer and solicited wisdom."

As I helped my daughter, Emileigh, pack up her dorm room at the end of her first college year, I found a stack of Valentine's Day cards I had sent to her.

"Oh, you still have some!" I exclaimed. "I love these! Did your friends like them?"

Crickets.

Thinking she hadn't heard me, I continued, "Were your friends amazed that you had *personalized* Valentines to give to them?"

My daughter, a very straight shooter, replied, "No. No, they didn't, because I never gave them out."

"What? Why? These are so fun! I mean, they are colorful, thoughtful, *and* they have your face in the middle of each one!"

"*Exactly*, Mom!" she said, emphatically. "Why in the world would I give my friends a Valentine's Day card with *my* photo on it? What am I, three years old?" she asked.

At first I was hurt. After all, I'd just wanted to help her connect with new friends. Was that so wrong? Didn't she know how much time it took to find just the right company with just the right card and just the right photo?

I looked at the cards again and started to chuckle. They were rather elementary. Truth be told, I'd missed her. I'd missed all the fun projects we used to do together. And I was struggling to find a good way to keep the communication going.

"A little over the top?" I asked.

"Just a little," she smirked.

We both began laughing, and I promised right then and there that I would not "help" her with future correspondence ideas.

She followed up with, "What were you thinking?"

"So many things," I said, as my voice tapered off.

She gave me a hug and said, "I appreciate the sentiment, but ask me next time."

"What? And ruin the surprise?" I exclaimed. We laughed again.

We finished packing and placed the final box in the car. In that moment, I realized how much of our connection had been hands-on, and that's why I was feeling the pain of her growing up. I'd used my hands. . .

to hold my child.
to feed my child.
to clothe my child.
to play with my child.
to protect my child.
to guide my child.
to connect with my child.

Our relationship had always been a tangible, act-and-react relationship. Whenever she'd needed something, I'd used my hands to help. Why, I'd even used my hands to make those unbelievably cool-only-to-mom Valentines! But through that experience, I also realized that connecting isn't only hands-on. Sometimes the most loving thing is to be hands-off and become a "guide on the side" who connects with our kids through prayer and solicited wisdom.

When I'm tempted to be too hands-on, I have to ask God to remind me of His care for my kids. That doesn't mean I disconnect; rather, it means I allow each of them space to grow into their own person and reliance on Jesus.

When our younger daughter, Aria, joined Emileigh at the same university, I had to learn these lessons all over again, which made me realize that the desire to do "hands-on" motherly things never ends and I have to find a way through transition.

Emileigh called me one day and said, "Did you really just text me to check on Aria, my sister, who lives in the same dorm on the same floor?"

At first I tried to defend myself. After all, I hadn't heard from Aria in two days. I live overseas.

I thought she might be too sick to lift her cell phone. I wanted to text my daughter back and ask, "Have you seen the movie *Taken* or that *Dateline* special on college stalkers?"

The imagination can create plenty of scenarios—including quicksand—that cause my "mother-radar" to go on alert. But once she read the text back to me, I realized it was a bit ridiculous.

As the years continue, I've learned to pause, rein in my worries, and most of all, pray. I love the way THE MESSAGE puts it:

> Don't fret or worry. Instead of worrying, pray. Let petitions and praises shape your worries into prayers, letting God know your concerns. Before you know it, a sense of God's wholeness, everything coming together for good, will

come and settle you down. It's wonderful what happens when Christ displaces worry at the center of your life. (PHILIPPIANS 4:6–7)

As I've given my children space and latitude to learn about adult living, they've given me cues to know how to meaningfully connect in ways that don't involve Valentine selfies. Here are a few examples:

Monday Memes. Each Monday in our Facebook family group, we send the funniest memes we can find. We compete to see who can find the best ones.

Saturday Sentinel. Because I work for a nonprofit in the Middle East, the time zone differences can make it tough to connect. So, every evening, I type a quick one- to two-sentence recap of the day's events. Then at the end of the week, I send it to the family so they can catch up when they have time.

Book Club. If we come across a good book, we'll tell the family about it. If it would generate good discussion, we set up times to chat about the book.

Purposed Family Vacations. Because our family lives in various places around the globe, we purpose dates to be together. We'll talk about potential locations, budgets, and so on, and then book a vacation rental. If we're not intentional, time will pass quickly and the "someday" will never happen.

Snail Mail. I don't know anyone who doesn't love getting mail (except bills). When I'm in the United States, I will purchase cards for birthdays, anniversaries, graduations, and anything else I can think of for the year. Then my husband and I will write notes in them, maybe include a gift card, and address them. A family member or friend will keep all these cards and mail them at the appropriate times.

Proof of Life. Sometimes when things are moving fast and connecting seems difficult, I'll request a "Proof of Life" photo. It's a funny, disarming way of letting them know that I'd like to make sure they're okay.

Over the years, I've had to adjust my methods based on the season my child was in. But no matter what, I didn't give up. So if you're wondering how to stay connected with kids who are trying to navigate life on their own, ask them how they'd like to communicate and how often. As you honor their requests, you'll find you'll connect better than ever. Pray and think about other ways you can stay connected to those who matter most, as long as it doesn't involve mailing a life-size cutout of yourself to remind them to call you.

—PAMELA J. MORTON, SPRINGFIELD, MISSOURI

Contentment Within

"I still needed more proof.
I needed to know that it was really God speaking
and not my own imagination."

My husband and I live and work in Tanzania as missionaries. Some years ago, when we were on sabbatical in the United States, our seven-year-old daughter was doing her homeschool studies and memorizing the Scripture that says, "I have learned, in whatsoever state I am, therewith to be content" (PHILIPPIANS 4:11 KJV).

Shortly after, we were driving from the East Coast to the West Coast and crossing each state line. At one point on the trip, our daughter exclaimed, "Now I get it! I have learned to be content in whatever *state* I am!" Of course we laughed at her well-timed joke. And even though we knew the Bible verse meant much more than that, our fun little incident was a good reminder that when we walk in obedience to the Lord, we can have contentment in spite of our circumstances.

Years earlier, we had been with the organization Youth With A Mission (YWAM) in Denmark. We'd been asked to continue on for another season of leading the Discipleship Training School. Our third daughter had been born about a year earlier, and I was just beginning to feel like we had a "normal life." Our oldest daughter, who had already moved four times in five years, was about to start kindergarten, and I was considering signing up for an evening class myself.

That's when my husband told me he felt the Lord was leading us to move on—to Africa. *No, no, no!* I thought. *It can't be!* All the arguments flooded my mind. After all, we were already serving in missions. We were training young people to go into the world and teach people the truth of God's Word. And most importantly, we were living in Denmark, my home country, for a change.

My husband decided to let the subject rest while he made a trip to the United States. Soon after, I started feeling ill. But with three kids and a discipleship class, where I was the interpreter for the visiting speakers, I had no time to be sick. Things got so bad I had to go see the doctor. He insisted on admitting me to the hospital immediately due to high infection numbers in my blood test.

"I can't," I told him. "My husband is away and my three kids need me."

He was persistent and said, "Well, as soon as he gets back, we need to get you properly checked out. Meanwhile, take this medication."

Less than a week later, I was admitted to the hospital, where they ran lots of tests, especially after learning I'd recently spent time in Africa. My family came to visit every day, which was really nice. But I was so tired, and I remember feeling happy to be able to rest and sleep without having any responsibilities for a little while. I also enjoyed having the opportunity to watch a royal wedding live on TV, which I wouldn't have been able to do at the YWAM base where we lived.

However, during that time in the hospital, the conversation I'd had with my husband lingered in the back of my mind. I contemplated whether the Lord was truly asking us to move on. I remembered a YWAM teaching about hearing the voice of God, about how to still your own voice and allow the Holy Spirit to speak to your heart and mind.

On the third day in the hospital, I had resorted to letting the Lord know why we *had* to stay in Denmark. For starters, I wanted to hold on to the proximity we had with my family. As a mom, I enjoyed seeing my kids with their grandparents. Not only that, but there were four other families serving at the YWAM base, and our children were so happy to have friends. Ultimately, our home in Denmark was a wonderful environment for all of us.

Along with these arguments, I had lots of concerns about moving—mostly involving my kids. Questions flooded my mind: Will they have friends? What about their schooling? Will they be safe? I was also in a moms' group of ladies who had all had babies within a month of each other. It felt like we had a lot in common and we had opportunities to pour into one another's lives. Needless to say, there were lots of tears as I wrote in my journal and finally found myself ready to be still and let the Lord have His say.

The wonderful thing is, God spoke gently to my heart. He reminded me that He loved me, loved my family, and was more concerned about their safety than I was. He reminded me of His faithfulness in the past and of the calling He had put on my life as well as my husband's. He reminded me that He can be trusted in all things and that He "shall gently lead those that are with young" (ISAIAH 40:11 KJV).

I cried again and repented of wanting my own way. But even though I understood the Lord was asking me to trust Him, that we were supposed to move into a new season of ministry, I still needed more proof. I needed to know that it was really God speaking and not my own imagination of what God would "probably" say. So I did something that I have only done maybe two or three times in my life. I asked the Lord to give me a Scripture reference to confirm what He had just impressed on my heart. Right away Exodus 33:11 came to mind. I had no idea what the words in the verse were, so I quickly looked it up. It said, "Inside the Tent of Meeting the LORD would speak to Moses face to face, as one speaks to a friend" (NLT).

The context of this verse is that whenever Moses went to inquire of the Lord, he would go to the tent of the tabernacle, the place where the Israelites offered sacrifices and worshiped God. But as I read it, the Lord impressed this on my heart: *The Lord speaks to me as one speaks to a friend.* Wow. What other confirmation did I need? Peace flooded my heart that day, and I thanked God for His guidance.

While I don't believe the Lord made me sick so He could speak to me, I know He allowed that compulsory time alone so I could quiet down and listen. That's why it's so important that we take time away to listen to the Lord, to get away from all the chaos so we can quiet our minds and hear what He has to say.

We did leave Denmark later that year to follow the Lord's call, and it has been a journey of highs and lows. I've often been thankful that He spoke so clearly to me back then and that His care and concern for my children truly is greater than my own. And, ultimately, I have learned in whatever *state* I am "therewith to be content."

—JETTE HALL, TANZANIA

I Want That Baby, Diego

"I just receive the comfort.
And I think of how perfectly she's embodying
Jesus' heart for me in this moment."

Another day, another friend announcing their pregnancy. I'm happy, yes. But I'm also hysterically crying on my bed while my kiddos splash around in the tub. Not my finest hour.

It had been almost nine months since I miscarried what would've been our third baby. It was actually two days before the due date. I know because I just checked my planner and saw the words "due date" scribbled out on the upcoming Sunday. I thought back to the summer months when I took the pregnancy test, got giddy over the positive test, dreamed of names, and saw how perfect the timing would be in the midst of our busy schedule. But here we are, two days away from March 10, and the only thing taking up space in my belly is the extra ten pounds I've gained from emotional eating the past nine months.

I think back to all the ups and downs of the last months. Trying to rationalize why it was no big deal that I miscarried. "There will be more opportunities; at least it happened early; it happens to lots of people; don't be dramatic." I worked hard to remain unaffected and power through the sadness. It wasn't my first rodeo—I miscarried in between my first and second pregnancies too. This time would be the same. I'd bleed for a while, wait a month, and get pregnant again. Boom.

But timing wasn't our friend over the next couple of months, and there were lots of weeks when my dear husband was out of town during *the week*. You know, that really fun time of the month when you're reading into every pang and ache on your right or left side trying to figure out when you're ovulating. Or subtly dropping hints all day that your husband better be ready that night. They never tell you how classy making babies can be.

Those months consisted of a lot of bargaining. *Give me the baby and I'll stop going to Starbucks so much. God, give me the baby and I swear I'll start waking up at six every morning to meet with You. Maybe if I make myself eat an egg every morning instead of sugary cereal, I'll get that baby!* Some days I sounded like the scary saber-toothed tiger from *Ice Age*: "I want that baby, Diego!" Watch out for the crazed lady eyeing all the babies on the street. She might not be stable.

I moved from bargaining to apathy, which really worked well. All the bad habits went through the roof since I was pretending I didn't care. "I'll eat this cookie and I'll eat three more. Because seriously, I don't care about when I have another baby. Whenever is fine. I'm happy. Look at me eating this cookie. Look how happy I am!" I don't think anyone bought that act.

And then came the pregnancy announcement. And then the next one. And the next. Something was seriously in the water. People were procreating at an alarming rate. The first few announcements were expected. I was sure I'd be pregnant soon, so no big deal. But as the months passed, the pregnancy announcements felt more and more like a slap on the face. Friends I had talked through the pain of waiting got their baby. And the friend who was all done having kids accidentally got another baby.

And here I sit. Alone on my bed. Crying hysterically. Coming face-to-face with what I was actually feeling: deep, deep longing and sadness.

All of a sudden my daughter stands up and yells, "Hey! Get me out of this tub so I can come over and wipe your tears."

I laugh, kind of embarrassed by my behavior but also touched by her words, and get her out of the tub. She cups my wet cheeks in her wet hands and wipes the tears away. She just sits. She has no words, just tender hands and a knowing gaze.

I just receive the comfort. And I think of how perfectly she is embodying Jesus' heart for me in this moment. No cliché phrases that diminish what I am feeling. No inspiring speeches about the resilience waiting brings. No pitying glances or diverted eye contact. Just complete and total willingness to be still with me.

I imagine that's how Jesus feels toward us in our waiting and our longing. He hurts with us. He longs with us. He waits with us. He wipes every tear. He looks us straight in the eye and chooses to walk with us through the moments of bargaining, apathy, frustration, grief, and pain. My tears start to subside, and I feel full of the peace that only comes when you're completely exposed. I realize all over again that He sees me and knows me and wants me still.

I walk over to get my daughter a towel (the tender tear wiping has ended, and she has started to whine about how cold she is). When I pick the towel off the floor, I look at my Bible verse calendar sitting on my dresser and read Zephaniah 3:17: "The Lord your God is with you" (NIV).

I get it, I get it, I get it. I feel overwhelmed by those little ways God meets me. In the uncharacteristically tender tear wiping of a child or an obviously placed Bible verse. Those moments give me hope—hope that I am promised intimacy with my Savior. An intimacy that produces peace and joy and contentment. And for today, I'll choose that.

Don't get me wrong; the crazy lady moments will almost definitely resurface. The longing, the hope, the grief—they're still there. But in this moment I choose to feel the warmth of a knowing God speaking love and peace over me through the gentle touch of my firstborn child.

—ELLE WILKERSON, WHEATON, ILLINOIS

A Child Like Peter

*"God's patience with Peter—and with you and me—
should encourage us to be persistent in loving,
understanding, and instructing our children."*

God has blessed me with two children, both boys. Now I was a tomboy when I was young, but that cannot prepare you to raise two boys—especially if they have attention deficit and hyperactivity disorder. Perhaps I should put *hyperactivity* in all caps!

Our oldest son is hyper, and when he was younger, he could watch TV, listen to all conversations in the house, and stand on his head at the same time. He is a sweet, personable kid (a young man today), but his disorder is real.

He is also all boy! My husband and I took a short walk on our street one day only to return to find an upstairs window open and our trampoline pulled close to the side of the house. What parent would not wonder, *What are you doing?* We thwarted the plan for his younger brother and him to—you guessed it—jump off the house to see how high they would bounce!

When he began missing his homework assignments at school (the beginning of many years of this), I suggested he use a piece of notebook paper in the front of his notebook to write down the homework assignments on the sheet. It made perfect sense to me. He said to me, "Mom, I know you want to help me, but that just doesn't work for me." I thought he was kidding, but he was not. So, he would write his assignments on his hand or arm and hope for the best. And he usually forgot to do his work, even if the marker stayed on his skin.

This began several years of me trying to help him and be his teacher's best friend. Believe me, the teacher needed a friend! I would go to teacher conferences, exchange emails, take phone calls, and follow up with his teacher.

On top of all this, my son loves to talk. As a child he also liked to fidget and get up often. Some teachers handled this well, but some did not, and one of the toughest situations occurred in kindergarten.

We had barely made it through two weeks of kindergarten when my son's teacher began to complain to me about my son's talking, moving, and inability to sleep or stay wiggle-free during nap time. Later I realized that this teacher also could use a few naps! She had her own set of struggles as a parent—including raising a teenage daughter. My son's talkative and hyper nature was not something she wanted to deal with during a school day.

As I was sharing my woes about kindergarten with my mom one day, she pulled out a small devotional book in which she had just read a devotion titled "A Child Like Peter." These words accompanied the devotion: "Peter was hurt because Jesus asked him the third time, 'Do you love Me?'" (JOHN 21:17 NIV). The word *hurt* stunned me. I had seen hurt in my son's eyes when my husband and I talked with him about his behavior. The hurt was the look of a child who was trying so hard and yet failing to be able to control himself. He so wanted to please us and his teacher, but his impulsive nature was difficult to control.

The devotion went on to ask if I had a child who seems to hear me only when he wants to. Yes, it seems that way.

Do I have to ask him the first time and then the second time to bring his homework home or to use his indoor voice? Does it seem that I must ask him three times? Yes, most often it did—sometimes four or fifteen times! Do I have a child like Peter? Yes, I do. Perhaps you do as well.

The apostle Peter denied his Lord three times (JOHN 18), even though he swore he would never do that (MATTHEW 26:35). In John 21:12–17 Jesus restored Peter's relationship with Him. Jesus asked Peter if he loved Him—three times. Later, in Acts 10, God repeated an important lesson to Peter three times.

It seems Peter was hard to convince. In Scripture he seems bold, loud, and impulsive. Just like my oldest son. God's patience with Peter encourages me to be patient with others, especially my son.

Do I always get this right? I would love to tell you yes, but since I first read that devotion all those years ago, I've read it again and again—and prayed and prayed for patience. Because I don't always get it right.

In Psalm 139:13–14, David wrote, "For You created my inmost being; You knit me together in my mother's womb. I praise You because I am fearfully and wonderfully made; Your works are wonderful, I know that full well" (NIV). What a beautiful reminder that God made us, He made our children, and He loves us all just as we are. He also loves us so much He does not want to leave us where we are! He wants us to grow, learn, and trust Him.

My son survived elementary, middle, and high school, and he is a college graduate. I am thankful for his accomplishments, even through the struggle of it all. He is now married to a beautiful young woman, and they have our first grandchild— our six-month-old baby girl. She looks just like her daddy did when he was her age. Oh, and she is already very wiggly! Could that be a sign? I do not know, but I will pray for her and her parents.

I have that devotional tucked into my Bible to this day, twenty-two years later. I cannot tell you how many times I have read it and reminded myself that I am like Peter. I can be bold, loud, and impulsive. I often forget things and repeat offenses, and I must go to my Father to ask for forgiveness—often three times or more.

So, do you have a child like Peter? Be encouraged, mom! God will go with you each step of the way. God's patience with Peter—and with you and me—should encourage us to be persistent in loving, understanding, and instructing our children.

And you know something? Peter turned out all right!

—LAWANDA TALLMAN, NEWNAN, GEORGIA

Chaos at Its Finest

*"Although my plans crumbled into chaos that day,
I was on God's trajectory."*

I often like to think I can do it all. And why not? I want to be successful, so I keep piling on the projects, ideas, and commitments. I'm fully engaged with life, touting the motto "How hard can it be?" I should have never asked.

It was an unusual September morning. The sun was shining, yet a light rain misted the ground. It was also the first day of school. My three darlings were heading back to yet another year of thrilling grade school education. My youngest child and only son, Tony, was now a big first grader, and that meant wearing the right clothes, having his hair smoothed back just so, and facing his biggest concern of all—riding the bus. To ease his fears, I told my little buddy I would drive him to the bus stop and wait with him there. It was a big day, indeed.

It was also a big day for me. I had agreed to teach a Bible class that started this same morning in a local church. In just a few minutes, I would be addressing more than two hundred women. Like Tony, I was more than a bit nervous.

The kids were scrambling as fast as they could, gobbling down cold cereal and drinking milk from the carton. So much for the steamy oatmeal and blueberry muffins I had planned. Max and Tiffany—the family dogs—positioned themselves under the chairs, snapping up every crumb that launched off the side of the table. I slapped peanut butter on hamburger buns, calling them a "special mom-creation sandwich," while simultaneously shouting, "Get your shoes on!" I loaded up the backpacks, kissed the girls goodbye, and scooted them out the door just in time for them to catch their middle school bus.

Yes! Two down.

Now for me. I ran to poof my hair and throw on my best Bible-teaching dress.

"Let's go Tony-boy," I rang out. "Time to catch your bus."

My big first grader and I scurried outside, swinging the door behind us shut, when we came to a dead stop. To our utter shock, several street construction workers were lined up with cranes and cones right behind my car. The roadwork down the street had progressed to the front of my house, and what once was a paved two-lane road was now a mud track.

We would have stood there all morning in disbelief, but the sound of the school bus jarred us out of our paralysis. There was no time to waste. "Let's move it out, son," I barked. Tony, in his new cowboy boots, and I, in my green stilettos, took off running through the mist and rain.

Potholes, dirt, sand, and puddles. I tried to avoid the mud-road land mines, but I was unsuccessful. My ankle folded over my high heel and I tumbled into a mud puddle, drenching my feet. Tony—who normally loves to splash in puddles—started to cry. He hated being late more than anything, except eating spinach.

We rounded the corner and made it just in time. I gave my tearful boy a secret squeeze (hugging him in public was not cool), and Tony climbed the steps and took his seat. My baby was off to school.

I would've had a mom moment, but there was no time for sentimentality. I could still get back to the house, change my clothes, re-poof my hair, and get the bulldozer to move so I could drive my car to church.

I spun around on my heels and headed for home when I noticed a black-and-white blur streak past my eyes like lightning. "Oh no, it's Tiffany," I bemoaned. My cocker spaniel was a runner and was never allowed outside unleashed. Now, like a prisoner making a jailbreak, Tiffany had managed to escape and was gallivanting wildly up and down the muddy two-track road.

Once more I took off running.

"Tiffany get back here," I demanded. "Come, girl! COME, right now!" I hollered for my aloof pooch as I chased after her. The more I ran, the faster she went, ears flopping in the wet morning breeze. I called her name, even offered treats, but once again that morning I was unsuccessful.

I was relieved when Mrs. Miller, my elderly next-door neighbor, opened her front door and offered some help. Only heaven knows how long she had been enjoying the morning chaos from her picture window. Tiffany pranced over to greet Mrs. Miller while I pounced without thinking and grabbed the muddy mutt by her collar. "Thank you so much, Mrs. Miller," I panted.

I made my way back home with dog in tow and gathered myself together. I had ten minutes before I was supposed to arrive at church. Fortunately, I lived only two minutes away, so getting there wasn't my problem. My concern was me. I looked like I'd been in a mud-wrestling match.

I frantically threw on my second-best Bible-teaching dress, whipped my hair into a ponytail and zoomed off to church. When I arrived, the worship center was full of exuberant women all excitedly chatting about the first day of school and their newfound freedom.

I took my place at the podium. "Hey, ladies, good morning! How great does this feel? Here we are together looking so refreshed and put together. But are there any moms out there who feel frazzled like I do this morning?" Hands raised all over the room, and the lilting sound of melodious laughter filled the air. I shared about my morning antics, and many affirming and empathetic women nodded their heads.

After the Bible class, an eighty-four-year-old woman hobbled over to me and slipped a piece of paper into my fist, patting my hand as she spoke. "Read it, honey; it will help you." Without looking I tucked the note in my pocket. But later that night I drew out the crumpled note and read the shaky script on the front: "How to Catch a Dog." I giggled as I opened it. Inside were these words:

> If you want to catch a dog, run in the opposite direction, laughing joyfully while calling the dog by name. The dog will turn and chase you home. Love, Eunice

Eunice Gunn's note blessed my heart, so I called her to thank her. "Oh honey, you're welcome. I'm glad this ole dog could help you with yours." Her unexpected humor once again made me giggle. We gabbed for several minutes about dogs and kids and Jesus.

The next week at Bible study, Eunice gave me a book titled *How to Train Your Dog*. Over the next few weeks a beautiful friendship blossomed. Eunice became a prayer partner, a confidant, a true grandmother in the faith. She joined my women's ministry team and began to teach other young women about the lessons of life she had learned through her walk with Jesus. Through her eyes I saw life from a new perspective.

I actually *had* been successful that brisk September morning. Although my plans crumbled into chaos that day, I was on God's trajectory: I made a wonderful friendship. My kids and I have a funny memory to share. I became transparent to other women who needed to know they weren't alone in their chaos. I learned how to train dogs. Most importantly, I learned how to laugh at life.

True success is found in recognizing the God-moments of life and yielding to His purpose in it all. I'm still overloaded in my schedule, but I am pursuing God's purpose for my life. He is in everything when I look for Him—chaos and all.

—DAWN SCOTT DAMON, ROCKFORD, MICHIGAN

Hide-and-Seek

*"Looking back now, I realize
I've always focused more on the joy of finding
than the dedication of seeking."*

There are always those dreaded moments—you know the ones. The moments when errands need to be run and things need to be accomplished but you endeavor to take your small children with you. If this thought makes you cringe, don't worry. You aren't alone. The thought of numerous stops, shuffling through multiple stores, and searching for that "necessary" little item brings on a level of anxiety only parents can define. That's why I say, "Bring on the treats, tablets, pre-shopping pep talks, and, yes, even bribes!"

Because of all the shopping hurdles my husband and I have jumped over in the past, we decided to get a little creative with our outings. We made the decision to turn our shopping trips into adventurous games of hide-and-seek. After all, what could be more fun than playing hide-and-seek at the store?

With two kids bursting with energy, it didn't take long for both of our children to get on board with our new shopping trip adventures. My daughter, who was three years old at the time, developed an uncanny ability for hiding well. My son, who is athletic and competitive, also played enthusiastically, often popping out of his hiding spot declaring, "Ha! You couldn't find me!" To him, the joy of hide-and-seek is more about the pursuit and the avoidance of becoming "it."

After testing out our new shopping game at a few different locations, we decided to up the ante. Why not play in the brand-new sporting goods store? There were so many new things to look at and plenty of aisles to explore. My husband decided to play the game with the kids while I scoured for the next season's gear. Bring on the kid-free shopping experience!

I can't tell you how many rounds of hide-and-seek they played before I was jolted out of my peaceful, kidless shopping fantasyland and had to help find our missing little princess. We split up and walked through the store, calling out her name while trying not to draw too much attention to ourselves. (No parent wants to be looked at as the one who has lost control of their kids!) However, our silent hide-and-seek Jedi wouldn't even let out a giggle. At first, we casually searched. But as time went on, our feet picked up the pace and our voices had the ring of desperation.

"Okay, we give up," we shouted. "You win!"

Silence. There wasn't a whimper, the pitter-patter of little feet, or a movement to reveal her location. I started to think of how my mother would have responded in this situation. She would start talking to everyone, speedily run through every aisle in a panic, and cry out to Jesus as she went. Once she located the kid, she would begin to weep and proclaim with reckless abandonment how good the Lord is, accompanied with full-on waterworks. But not me. I am cool as a cucumber.

Years of management experience at an amusement park and retail store have given me the ability to think rationally and avoid freaking out in difficult situations. I am methodical in my problem solving, so I'm able to remain calm. My husband, on the other hand, isn't so calm. So in our nowhere-to-be-found daughter situation, he shamelessly resorted to bribes.

"You're the best hider! You win! Come get your prize! Want some candy?"

Eventually, we found her in a rack I was sure I had already checked. She had climbed up on the cross beam and we only found her when we peered down the middle of it. There she was—encircled by a rack of pro-sport team attire, full of smiles with her bright sparkling brown eyes and head full of curls.

"Ta-da!" she said. "Now do I get my candy?" She was completely oblivious to how terrified we had been in our search for her. We grabbed her, hugged her, kissed her, and tenderly brushed back those luscious curls. Then, we looked right into those big brown eyes and let her know that she gave us the scare of a lifetime. It was time to rethink our adventurous shopping tactics!

Looking back, I realize I've always focused more on the joy of finding than the dedication of seeking. However, as I recounted the events of that day, I was reminded of the parable of a woman in the Bible who had lost a coin and searched and searched until she found it.

Luke 15:8-9 says, "Suppose a woman has ten silver coins and loses one. Won't she light a lamp and sweep the entire house and search carefully until she finds it? And when she finds it, she will call in her friends and neighbors and say, 'Rejoice with me because I have found my lost coin'" (NLT).

While I know this parable focuses on God's heart to seek after people who belong in His kingdom, I can't help but think of all the other Scripture passages that encourage us to seek tirelessly after Him and His righteousness. In all honesty, there have been times in my life when I've given less than the lost coin effort in my pursuit of God. A quick little prayer, a rushed little devo, and a distracted worship service have been all I've given in seeking the Lord. But isn't He worth more than that? Where is that sweep-every-crumb, leave-no-cushion-unturned, I'm-not-leaving-till-I-find-you type of commitment to the Lord?

There was no way I was leaving that sporting goods store without my little girl that day. After all, I treasure my kids. So, how much more should I treasure my Lord? As an encouragement to all of us, in life's game of hide-and-seek, let's keep seeking the One who can always be found. Let's pursue His kingdom and His righteousness above all else. It's a pursuit that is definitely worthwhile—and much better than a candy reward in the end.

—MICHELLE BEEDLE, WINTER GARDEN, FLORIDA

The Loser Mom Club

*"Moms are the first to show grace to others
and the last to let themselves off the hook."*

Before having children, no one told me that motherhood is like entering a brutal match of comparison with other moms. It's a competition to see who is doing it best. At first, I tried to win—I really did. I was a baseboard-scrubbing, home-keeping zealot! I dressed my three boys and baby girl in coordinating church outfits, and (most nights) had dinner ready by 6:00 p.m. But sometime after the birth of boy #3, it became as obvious as the buildup of dry shampoo in my hair that this self-inflicted competition wasn't sustainable. So, I did the unthinkable—I embraced losing.

Not only that, I even formed a squad—the Loser Mom Club. We encouraged one another to set our bars low. My friends and I regularly shared our latest failures to see who earned the role of "President" that week. Their stories usually consisted of things such as forgetting to send lunch money or not fixing their daughter's hair for school pictures. I considered my friends amateurs.

After all, no one has surpassed the time I forgot to pick up my boys from summer camp. That incident made me "President of the Loser Mom Club" forever. No term limits.

You might be asking how on earth I could forget my kids—and their friend—at summer camp. Well, this camp had a girls' camp one week and a separate boys' camp the next.

The girls' camp was publicized as Monday through Friday, and for some reason it never occurred to me that the boys' camp would have a different schedule. The brochure said nothing about picking the boys up on Thursday. Whoever created it must not understand the life of a frazzled mom!

Anyway, the infamous camp week had been relatively peaceful with two of our boys away. I took advantage of the calm to organize my coupon binder and make an epic trip to the grocery store where I double-couponed to my heart's content. As I rolled into the unfortunate cashier's lane to begin sorting my purchases, my cell phone rang.

Son: "Mom, where are you?"

Me: "Hey! I'm at the store. How's camp?"

Son: "When are you getting here? We are the last kids. Everyone else has been picked up."

Me: Silence

I can't tell you what I said next because I blacked out. I'm sure it was something like, "But, it's not Friday yet, so why is everyone going home?" and "What do you mean camp is over on a Thursday when everyone knows CAMP ALWAYS ENDS ON FRIDAY!" and "Please forgive me, buddy. I'm on my way. Please put the camp director on the phone."

I vaguely remember trying to contain my hysteria and speaking with the camp director saying, "Mr. Director, I am *so* sorry. Can you ever forgive me? Can you please take care of them just a bit longer—like two-and-a-half hours longer? Maybe feed them some lunch until I get there?"

During this whole panicked conversation, I was still in the checkout line. The look that the cashier was giving me screamed, "Go to another line, lady! *Please* go to another line!" At that very moment, I stumbled and dropped my gargantuan binder. Coupons flew through the air like ticker tape at a Wall Street parade.

I looked at the mess on the floor and my huge cart of "bargains" that I never would have bought without the coupons, and saw that the cashier was as stunned as I've ever seen another human being (short of witnessing a crime). She broke my gaze and scanned my goods like someone competing for "Fastest Ringer-Upper." I paid double my food budget and ran out the door even faster.

With the car loaded, I sank into the driver's seat and sobbed. I delivered a left hook after a right jab of self-loathing to my already broken heart for being so inexplicably stupid. That's when my phone rang again. It was my friend, whose son I was also supposed to pick up at camp. I waited for the blows to come, for being so irresponsible with her son, but do you know what I received instead? Grace.

She was completely understanding while I stuttered through my lame excuses. "It could happen to anyone!" she said. (Seriously? Name one.) It just so happened her husband was leaving work and offered to get the boys. And then she said the most comforting thing of all: "It's going to be alright."

I've thought about that event many times and wondered how I can extend grace more freely to myself and others. Here's what I've realized: moms are the first to show grace to others and the last to let themselves off the hook. I've mentally bashed myself for being such a negligent parent time and time again. But here's the deal: Had it been my friend rather than me who forgot the kids at camp, I wouldn't have added injury to insult. I wouldn't have told her what a loser mom she was. And I certainly wouldn't have told her that her kids would be lucky to escape their adolescence without therapy if she didn't pull it together! I've realized we must extend the same grace to ourselves that we would give to someone else facing their own inadequacies. We moms won't survive the mental anguish otherwise.

You see, grace defaults to believing the best about someone and understands intent even when the follow-through is lacking. Grace also laughs instead of becoming bitter. Why? Because we know the love that undergirds grace assures us that most people don't try to hurt us intentionally. First Peter 4:8 tells us, "Above all, love each other deeply, because love covers a multitude of sins" (NIV). And I Corinthians 13 captures this kind of love in verse 5: "[Love] is not easily angered, it keeps no record of wrongs" (NIV).

It's critical for every mom to find her "squad" who shares a love for God and will be a source of protection instead of competition. When a mom can remove her focus from winning, she is free to embrace losing. And that's when the undeserved, unmerited arms of grace wrap around her and assure her, "It's going to be alright."

—LISA MCKAY, HENAGAR, ALABAMA

Spirited Sprouts

*"I realized I had a few bean sprouts myself—
and not the garden variety. They were real-life sprouts
that I want to love and nurture."*

My daughter came home from school today, proud to share with me the contents of a crumpled-up piece of tissue paper. And you know what? I almost missed it. In fact, I almost dismissed it, both the moment and the meaning. I was too preoccupied to pay much attention to the tissue paper or to the contents it held. Of course, this is easy for any mom to do, including me—a mom to ten children. (Yes, ten!) All moms get caught up in the macaroni boiling on the stove, the events that need to be written on the calendar, and the dryer buzzer going off (all at once, mind you). But that day I was extra distracted, having spent much of the afternoon contemplating different writing topics for a project I was working on. It's not that I didn't have anything to write about; I had some heavy themes about death and dying, dashed expectations, and extended family moving. But none of it was clicking.

In fact, earlier in the day, I had posted a social media status about my need for inspiration, and then I'd pondered the response from an old friend now living in Venice. He had basically accused me of being up to my armpits in inspiration, living with an abundance of it. In fact, he'd added, "You're one lucky lady" (or something like that).

I contemplated the word *inspiration* in Italian: *ispirazione*, which means "to breathe into."

Instantly, I thought about my spirited children, the ones I should eagerly pay attention to, the ones who bring more inspiration than I could ever ask for. Dropping my writing project, I went to find my daughter with her crumpled-up tissue. Where had she gone?

"Merryn!" I called but heard no answer.

Hmmm. Left behind on the kitchen counter was a plastic, oversized 101 Dalmatians souvenir cup. I recalled it had been nearly eight years earlier when I took our oldest daughter to see Disney on Ice. She had been thrilled to receive the cup that night, clutching the treasure in her little hands, all the while recounting the memories of a magical evening.

Why do we even still have this around? I thought. *It fits awkwardly in the dishwasher. It fits awkwardly in the cabinet.* Very likely, the snow cone it held, which was an exorbitant $15, was the reason I was still trying to get my money's worth out of it. I was ready to toss the empty cup into the sink when I looked into the bottom. Inside was a little pinto bean. Now, where did that come from?

My daughter Merryn reentered the kitchen and noticed the Dalmation cup in my hand. "Mom," she said. "Look at that! When the seed opens up, you can see part of the root. That means it's growing! Oh, and look how it's germinating! This means we can plant it!" At that moment, I actually marveled at the fascinating seed, the two symmetrical pieces, the tiny root, the bitty stem, the little leaf all growing inside. It's all there, waiting for the right mix of dirt and nurturing, attention and warmth. Like ideas. Like children.

I quickly got diverted again by an unopened piece of mail and overflowing backpacks strewn about. When I finally happened to glance out my kitchen window, I saw her. She hadn't even changed out of her school uniform before she'd successfully found a large shovel from the garage and was wrestling with it against the hard ground below. There she was, digging a hole right in the middle of the backyard with a furrowed brow and a big smile on her round face.

I was moved to get closer because her enthusiasm drew me in. I genuinely wanted to see this process of digging, planting, and growing. Not even stopping to slip on shoes, I turned off the stove and headed outside. It occurred to me that this child was clearly inspired. She was excited about what she was learning, eager to put her thoughts into words and share them with me. She was making connections and applying them to her world. Her self-starting, can-do attitude didn't wait for a mom easily distracted by phone calls, or a mom who might have gotten preoccupied with gardening protocol. She didn't consult books about how far apart to plant, where the best sunbeams would land at midday, or the importance of drainage or soil acidity. I marveled at her confidence. Even more, I was awed by her sense of hope that if she planted a seed, it would grow—even if that planted seed was literally in the middle of a backyard with a dozen children running through it.

Right there in the middle of my backyard, barefoot on the grass, I realized I had a few bean sprouts myself—and not the garden variety. They were real-life sprouts that I want to love and nurture. Little sprouts who were meant to grow and yield a fruitful harvest. I had to stop and ask myself the question, "What kind of garden have I been cultivating?" I thought of all the growing moments I'd missed because I hadn't been attentive. I felt sad about the distractions I'd allowed to take the place of wonderment.

When I finally sat down at the computer and started

writing again, it came a little easier once I started paying attention to my true inspiration. Grow, little seeds. Grow. As I wrote, my thoughts turned to Matthew 13:23: "But he who received seed on the good ground is he who hears the word and understands it, who indeed bears fruit and produces: some a hundredfold, some sixty, some thirty" (NKJV).

A few chapters later, we read that the disciples approached Jesus and asked, "'Who then is the greatest in the kingdom of heaven?' Then Jesus called a little child to Him, set him in the midst of them, and said, 'Assuredly, I say to you, unless you are converted and become as little children, you will by no means enter the kingdom of heaven. Therefore whoever humbles himself as this little child is the greatest in the kingdom of heaven. Whoever receives one little child like this in My name receives Me'" (MATTHEW 18:1–5 NKJV).

These passages inspire me to stop and welcome the children in my midst. Instead of distractedly listening, I want to receive every precious experience they bring—tiny bean sprouts and all.

—KELLY KRENZ, CHENOA, ILLINOIS

Cheese Sauce

*"I didn't want to settle for obligatory motions
of static prayers or forced 'shoulds' in my spiritual life,
and I didn't want my kids to settle for that
in their spiritual lives either."*

When I became a mom, it was important to me to model and teach my kids how to develop a fluent and fluid relationship with God. Just as I had learned to do in my adult life, I attempted to make each day a continual conversation with God, thanking and praising Him for the things I encountered. I didn't want to settle for obligatory motions of static prayers or forced "shoulds" in my spiritual life, and I didn't want my kids to settle for that in their spiritual lives either. I wanted an intimate relationship—an all-day, every day, fluid, back-and-forth relationship with God full of gratitude, respect, awe, and deep love for Him. I wanted my kids to know how to have this kind of relationship with God as well.

As a result of this hope for my children, I started teaching them when they were babies and toddlers about the fluency of relationship we could have with our Creator. Whenever we saw the moon in the night sky and one of the kids squealed, "*Look!* There's the moon!" I'd always follow that up with an excited, "Wow! What do we say to Jesus?" I'd teach them words broken up into easy-to-remember syllables like "Thank-You-Je-sus-for-the-moon." To this day, if I ask my eleven-year-old son, "What do we say about the moon?"

he will smirk and repeat the phrase back to me in a semi-annoyed way. (As a tween, most things that come out of his mouth are spoken with an underlying degree of annoyance.)

I also taught my kids to stop and pray for anyone who got hurt. We prayed for accidents on the road as we drove past, for stray animals running wild, and for ambulances, fire trucks, and police officers as they sped by. We prayed and thanked God for the sunsets, the rare occasions of snow in Memphis, upcoming tests, and good grades.

Of course, there were times when the kids weren't so thankful. For example, one day our four-year-old son Ryan was overtired. We were running errands in the morning, and it had taken longer than I had anticipated. I was racing around town as quickly as I could to finish up the last few errands on our way home. Ryan was having a full-blown meltdown in his car seat because he needed a nap after staying up too late the night before. I decided to point his thoughts toward gratitude by saying, "Thank You, Jesus, for this beautiful day!" He replied with a guttural, raging, and furious response, "NO THANK YOU, JESUS!"

Still other times, my mother-heart is warmed when I hear my kids thank the Lord as their first response. My nine-year-old daughter once jumped in the minivan and told me about how a troubled girl in her class who had a long reputation of getting in trouble "was having a better year because Jesus is really changing her." Another time, a mom of one of my son's best friends called me to say that our boys regularly asked the other to pray. Instinctively, my children have said "Praise God!" or "Thank You, God!" when they have received good news.

Last year, my otherwise healthy husband got the flu, which turned into double pneumonia within a couple of days. He was hospitalized, intubated a day later, and quickly went into complete lung failure. He was on life support for weeks and in the ICU for two months. The children weren't allowed to see him, and with all the tubes, wires, and machines, I really didn't want them to. I let them write notes, draw pictures, and send messages to him through me.

One evening, well into the second month of his life support in the ICU, my then eight-year-old daughter asked if she could record a video on my phone for her daddy. I agreed, so she grabbed my cell phone and disappeared to the corner of the dining room where she could hide out next to the buffet to record a video message for him. A day or two later, I remembered her video message and pulled out my phone to see what she had recorded for her dad. With a wobbly phone held close to her face, capturing her hot pink glasses, she spoke words of faith and healing to her daddy. She quoted Jeremiah 29:11 from memory: "'For I know the plans I have for you,' declares the LORD, 'plans to prosper you and not to harm you, plans to give you hope and a future'" (NIV).

Then she talked for a minute or two about how God wouldn't have put that verse in His Word if He didn't mean it to include her dad. She was full of faith on the video, assuring her daddy that God was going to heal him. I was speechless. (And God did, in fact, heal him.)

These example show how this modeling and teaching a fluid relationship with God has produced fruit, but at other times my attempts as a mom have failed, and I am certain I have managed to mess up my kids' understanding of who God is. For example, when my oldest son had just turned two, we were on our way to the grocery store to pick up a few things. This is the exchange that occurred in the car:

Andrew: "Andrew loves cheese sauce."

Me: (Thinking of how much we both love cheese) "Momma loves cheese sauce, too. Cheese sauce is delicious!"

Andrew: Silence

Me: "We love cheese sauce on chips, with salsa, and on broccoli, don't we?"

Pulling into the grocery store parking lot, Andrew sat in his seat with a confused look on his face. Then he looked at me and said, "Mary, Joseph, and cheese sauce?"

It was then I realized he was saying *Je-sus*, not cheese sauce. Laughing, I pulled him out of his car seat and said, "Well, never mind the broccoli thing then."

The Bible tells us in Psalm 139:2 that God knows our thoughts. Jesus also tells us in John 15:15 that He calls us friends. What beauty I find because of the personal relationship we can have with God. Whether my kids' first response is "Praise the Lord" or "I love Cheese Sauce," I know that our Lord knows their thoughts and He is worshiped just the same.

—SARAH BISHOP, ARLINGTON, TENNESSEE

One of Those Days

*"Her bad day was spreading over the family worse
than pink eye in a kindergarten class.
And the truth was, we were all riding
the struggle bus with no exit in sight."*

A s a mom, have you ever had "one of those days"? Surely, you know the days I'm talking about. The day when everyone is fighting, nothing is going right, and you feel like you are losing your mind. That was me about a month into the COVID-19 quarantine. It literally felt like *Groundhog Day* because it was a direct repeat of the day before. I had lost my sense of rhythm and routine, as my poor kids were suddenly pulled from school and thrust into online learning—which only added to the crazy. Needless to say, it was a stressful time for all of us.

My very social youngest, a first grader who loves school and was desperately missing her routine, woke up one morning having one of her own struggle-bus days. She was grumpy, couldn't find anything good for breakfast, thought her older sister was being mean, and found her brother to be annoying. She was even convinced the dog didn't like her!

I tried coaxing her into doing schoolwork, but she complained that she had no good books to read, writing was boring, and her math problems were confusing. By lunchtime, I was *so* over it. In fact, I had been over it within ten minutes of the day starting! Her bad day was spreading over the family worse than pink eye in a kindergarten class.

And the truth was, we were all riding the struggle bus with no exit in sight.

After a few quick prayers, I realized she just needed some one-on-one attention and a change of scenery. So, I asked her to take the dog (the one that hated her) on a short walk with me. I figured some fresh air would do us both some good. Thankfully, she didn't put up too much of a fight. It took about three minutes of walking quietly before the floodgates opened! I can't even begin to explain to you the five hundred different topics she covered during that thirty-minute walk. After all, she had my undivided attention and she had things to say! She told me about friends and favorite colors and about how she wanted to go swimming in the summer. It was as if she opened up her little heart and spilled out all its contents.

As we were walking, I found myself tearing up. I was absolutely mesmerized by her little seven-year-old self. Her brown hair was in a ponytail that was swaying back and forth as she walked. She'd look at me and smile when she was telling me something funny, and I found myself loving every precious moment. As we walked, she told me about things that seemed so big and important to her but seemed insignificant to me. As I watched my daughter picking random dandelions out of yards and chatting away, the Holy Spirit spoke to my heart and reminded me that God delights in us. Psalm 149:4 says, "The LORD delights in His people" (NLT).

In fact, the God of the universe delights in us so much that He longs for us to stop what we are doing and walk with Him. He wants us to converse with Him and to tell Him all about our problems. Similar to how I viewed my daughter's concerns, God sees our problems as small compared to His sovereignty, but He doesn't mock us or treat us as if they aren't important. Every word my daughter said drew my heart to listen to her. It's like that with God; He *wants* to listen to us as we tell Him how we feel and what is troubling us.

Whenever I feel down, I love to read the Psalms for encouragement. In Psalm 18, David sang a song to the Lord after God rescued him from his enemy, Saul. In verse 19, David wrote, "He led me to a place of safety; He rescued me because He delights in me" (NLT).

What a beautiful reminder of our loving, attentive God. Because He delights in us, He pays attention to what concerns us. The big things, the small things, the repetitive Groundhog-Day things. God cares about everything we go through.

As we neared the end of our walk that day, the Holy Spirit spoke another truth to my heart: Our whole countenance can change when we take our cares and concerns to God. Because I'd taken time out of my day to give my daughter my undivided attention, her entire countenance and attitude had changed for the better. She went from grumpy to gracious in less than thirty minutes! I don't know about you, but I sure could use that kind of turnaround some days. By simply pouring out her heart to me, talking about everything and nothing at the same time, the weight of worry and discontentment lifted from her tiny shoulders. She literally walked back into our home feeling lighter and happier.

My dear friend, the next time you're having "one of those days," give yourself pause and take a walk with God. Open up to Him about every single thing on your mind. In fact, as you are walking, envision God walking beside you, delighting in the person He created you to be. After all, you are His child!

No matter how old (or cranky) my kids get, they are still my kids and I love them to pieces. And no matter how old we get, God is there to listen. He delights in us when we pour our hearts out to Him. And within a matter of minutes, our walk with the Lord will help us feel lighter than we did before. Then, as we return to some semblance of our routine—even in periods of quarantine—we'll be able to approach it with a much calmer, happier attitude than before.

—CINDY BILLER, GRAND HAVEN, MICHIGAN

The Value of Other Mamas

*"As vulnerable as it may feel,
there is a longing to be loved and cared for
by other mamas, because God created us
to experience these relationships."*

It was one of those "mom moments" that was a panic attack in the making. For months and months, I had locked my infant and toddler in the bathroom with me while I showered. However, as they grew, they began to exercise their independence and no longer wanted to be locked in the steamy bathroom. One day I bravely decided to let both of my children rule the house while I took a quick shower. It was so quick, I'm not even positive my body got cleaned that well. As I turned on the water, my mind raced with all the things my toddlers could be doing. I quickly jumped out of the shower, barely wet, and wrapped a towel around my body so I could poke my head out and make sure those angelic children were still sitting quietly in front of the TV.

These shower-at-your-own-risk moments went without a hitch most days, as my sweet children were safely engrossed in *Blue's Clues*. But one particular morning, I hurried through my shower to find my youngest daughter with dirt all over her chin and around her mouth. Immediately, I felt panic grip my body.

I looked at my son and asked, "Conner, what happened to Chloe? Why does she have dirt all over her face?" I tried to speak calmly, but my heart was racing. My sweet four-year-old looked at me with the sincerest eyes and responded, "I was pretending Chloe was my puppy dog, and I fed her dirt." (They must have been watching *Blue's Clues* that day!)

I asked where the dirt had come from and found out it was the potting soil from one of my potted plants. This soil was no ordinary ground dirt. It was full of Miracle Grow, peat moss, and who knows what else! Fear overwhelmed my heart. *What do I do? Is this potting soil going to make her sick? Do I call the doctor? Poison control?* I didn't know what to do! I decided to call a close friend and ask her advice. I would like to say that this was the only time in my life that my rational thinking was overshadowed by overwhelming panic. But it wasn't. I've desperately needed other women to speak wisdom into many situations throughout my life.

Fast-forward several years, and my son had just turned eighteen. One day, I noticed two bandages on his fingers and asked what had happened. He sheepishly responded, "Mom, don't even ask." Knowing boys will be boys, I asked nothing further. But I was certain he had done something not-so-smart.

About a week after this conversation and only a few days before he started his freshman year of college, he showed me a red splotch on his upper arm and asked if I knew what it was. It was concerning, but once again I didn't have a clue. Trying not to panic, I stated he would need to see a doctor if it didn't get any better. I proceeded to the kitchen to begin dinner preparations. A few minutes later, my not-so-angelic teenager asked, "Mom, could that red splotch on my arm be related to my fingers?" I gasped when I saw that one of his fingers was severely infected from a burn! Needless to say, dinner preparations ceased. I immediately took my son to the emergency room, where he received a dose of intravenous antibiotics and a prescription to continue at home. I continued to watch his finger and arm, but I saw no improvement. I was sure it was worsening.

On the morning of his first day of college, I was filled with concern. Every blood vessel in his arm, up through his shoulder and into his chest, was raised and fire-engine red. There were traceable red lines all over his body that weren't from a permanent marker! However, his nonchalant response was not in agreement with my worry. I wanted to take him to the doctor immediately, but he wanted to go through his first day of classes and then go to the doctor that afternoon. Questions filled my mind. *What do I do? Do I make him miss his first day of college? Do I let him wait until the afternoon? How sick is he?* Tears came to my eyes as I tried to sort out what the best decision was. My mama's heart was torn and fearful. I called a friend, who immediately advised me to take my son to the ER. When I gave her reasons why I didn't want him to miss his first day of college, she replied, "I am on my way to your house, and I will make you both go to the ER because I love you."

As moms, we will continually find ourselves in situations in which we need someone to connect with to shed light on our lives and to love us well. Scripture tells us in I Thessalonians 5:11, "Therefore encourage one another and build one another up, just as you are doing" (ESV).

As vulnerable as it may feel, there is a longing to be loved and cared for by other mamas, because God created us to experience these relationships. Not only do we need other women for moments when we don't know what to do, but also we need other women to share our struggles and successes.

The morning I found myself in my living room wondering

whether I needed to call poison control for my daughter, I needed to call a friend who could calm my spirit and assure me a little potting soil was most likely not going to make her sick. The morning I stood in the bathroom with my eighteen-year-old son debating if I should spoil his first day of college, I needed a friend who loved me and could speak the hard truth to me.

And guess what? My daughter was fine. The potting soil digested well. My son spent three days in the hospital getting intravenous antibiotics and missing his first week of college. We survived the ordeals but only because relationships along the way helped me get through them.

You may be asking, "How do I find time to develop relationships so that when situations arise, I will have a sweet friend to reach out to?" I believe it begins with intentionality. Intentionally go on lunch dates. Intentionally go on walks together. Pay attention to what is going on in your friends' lives and be available to them. In different seasons of life, we have different friends. And that's okay. Be willing to release friends and make new ones at the same time. It's crucial to healthy friendships. Most of all, trust God with your relationships, and be vulnerable enough to share your heart with the people God has placed in your life. After all, we need the Lord and we need each other.

—KAREN SMITH, MADISON, ALABAMA

Give Me That Mountain

"I wonder what other amazing things I miss out on because I choose to listen to the wrong voice."

Did you know there are more than 365 reminders in the Bible that tell us not to be afraid? That's at least one reminder for every day of the year! We tell our children not to be afraid. We share stories with them about brave Bible warriors who charged into battle and were victorious because God was with them. And we encourage our kids to imagine that they are like those courageous men and women who overcome life's battles with God's help.

A couple of months ago, I came to a realization that I was not as brave as I thought I was. My sons were discussing how much schoolwork they had left to do and how they didn't have much time to finish it. I could tell they were feeling stressed and overwhelmed, so I quickly came up with what I thought was a brilliant analogy to encourage them.

I said, "Okay, guys, listen up. You know when we go skiing, and we are at the very top of the mountain looking down at the steep slope? Well, you don't just look at the bottom of the mountain, point your skis downward, and go for it. That would be too overwhelming! Instead, you look a couple of feet ahead of you and ski little by little until you make it all the way down. Well, that's how you are going to finish your schoolwork. Don't look at the big stack of assignments in front of you. Look at one assignment at a time and move your way forward bit by bit. Soon, all your schoolwork will be done and you will successfully reach the bottom of the slope!"

Of course, I thought it was the perfect word picture, but the boys just stared at me with confused looks on their faces. Even my husband gave me a blank stare. I tried to explain my analogy once again, but it still wasn't clicking. Finally, my husband said, "We don't think about stuff like that when we go skiing. We literally point our skis downward and go!"

I was stunned. After all, I thought everyone skied like me! When I am at the top of the mountain looking down, tons of thoughts circle around in my head. Those thoughts tell me how dangerous skiing is. They remind me of the million ways I can get hurt. And they shout warnings about how I don't belong up there on top of the mountain. When I'm looking down the slope, I recall every story I've ever heard about people dying while skiing. Even when I've skied the same mountain ten times, that voice of fear gets louder and louder each time, and the skiing becomes less and less enjoyable.

That day, I realized my husband and children did not have the same thoughts that I did. And they certainly weren't as afraid as I was. In fact, they reminded me of Joshua and Caleb from the Bible. They were two of the twelve men chosen to spy out the land of Canaan—the hill country flowing with milk and honey—and the very land that God had promised the people of Israel. God said He would be with them, and Joshua and Caleb remembered that promise! Although the other spies returned from Canaan in fear and trembling, Joshua and Caleb kept their eyes on God's provision. While everyone else saw giants and obstacles, Joshua and Caleb saw the hand of God. They said to the people of Israel, "The land we traveled through and explored is a wonderful land! And if the LORD is pleased with us, He will bring us safely into that land and give it to us. It is a rich land flowing with milk and honey. Do not rebel against the LORD, and don't be afraid of the people of the land. They are only helpless prey to us! They have no protection, but the LORD is with us! Don't be afraid of them!" (NUMBERS 14:7–9 NLT).

I see now that my boys are like Joshua and Caleb. When they are skiing on the mountain, they are not afraid. They have childlike faith and trust. If their dad tells them they can do it, they believe him. If he tells them he will be right by their side, they don't question him. When he says they are going to have an amazing day, they do! It doesn't matter how difficult the run is, they are fully confident that with their dad's help, they will successfully make it down the slope (in one piece).

Pondering this analogy and my own fear of skiing, I wonder what other amazing things I miss out on because I choose to listen to the wrong voice. The thing is, God does not want us to live in fear; He wants us to walk in faith and trust in Him. He is a good Father and promises to be with us always. He wants us to have a clear perspective and enjoy life to its fullest. The same God who parted the Red Sea and allowed the people of Israel to cross on dry ground promises to take care of us, too!

I don't know about you, but I want to trust my Father just like Joshua and Caleb did. I want to be someone who wholeheartedly follows after God with great faith and a spirit set apart for Him. So, from now on, I'm making this promise to myself: No longer will I let fear get in the way. No longer will I let doubt hold me back. I might still have fearful thoughts that remind me of how dangerous the slope is, but I'll replace those thoughts with God's promises. And, I'll trust that my heavenly Father is with me every inch of the way. Now, give me that mountain!

—JENNIFER FEHR, MARTENSVILLE, SASKATCHEWAN, CANADA

Seen and Loved

"I wasn't prepared for how often I would feel invisible."

All I can say about those first years of motherhood is "wow." As a mom of two preschool-aged children, I have not yet reached the stage of looking back on those first months with rose-colored glasses. Don't get me wrong; I love my girls. They are the best! But when I see a fellow mom at the grocery store struggling to keep a toddler entertained, fill the cart with groceries, and deal with her sleeping (or more likely screaming) infant in the car seat, I don't immediately wish myself back in her shoes.

As a teenager, I babysat every chance I got. I took jobs that required taking care of young children, such as camp counselor and daycare teacher. I majored in early childhood education because I loved kids and couldn't wait to have little people of my own. But I wasn't prepared for how often I would feel invisible. I wasn't at all prepared for the sleep deprivation, the constant demands, and the pressure to be a really good mom. Honestly, those pressures began planting seeds of doubt in my mind. I began to ask questions such as *Does God even see me? Has my life suddenly been reduced to nanny, cook, and laundress?*

Before kids, I had been an integral part of a college ministry team with Cru (formerly called Campus Crusade for Christ). I had shared the gospel, mentored young women, and worked on important projects. One of those projects involved planning 5k races to bring freedom to those in brothels across the globe. But once I had kids, I found I couldn't even make it through a Sunday sermon without having to leave with a fussy child in tow. If I ever found the time to sit down with my Bible, I would usually fall asleep before I could think about what the passage was saying, much less interpret or apply it to my life.

The effects of sleep deprivation, along with a series of huge transitions in our family, left me feeling overwhelmed and unsure of my own faith. Again, condemning thoughts assaulted my mind: *You're a missionary, and you can't even find time to spend with the Lord! Doesn't that make you a hypocrite? You shouldn't be on staff at all!*

These were the lies that plagued me over and over again. Of course, if I had been open about these struggles, I would have quickly learned how normal they were—how other mothers in ministry had the same feelings. But I thought it was just me, so I trudged on, not wanting anyone to know how much I was struggling.

However, God knew exactly how I was feeling. And in just the right way, at just the right time, He comforted me from His Word. I'm not even sure when, exactly, this particular passage in Isaiah got underlined in my Bible, but when I came across it again, it seemed to leap off the page. It says, "Behold, the Lord GOD comes with might, and his arm rules for him; behold, his reward is with him, and his recompense before him. He will tend his flock like a shepherd; he will gather the lambs in his arms; he will carry them in his bosom, and gently lead those that are with young" (ISAIAH 40:10–11 ESV).

As I reread the underlined passage, I couldn't help but be overwhelmed with God's love and truth. My mind was filled with awe. Do you mean to tell me that the same God who made the heavens and earth sees ME— little ol' me in all my unshowered, hot mess? Does the God of the universe really promise to be gentle with me—a mom of young children? Oh, how that passage was water to my thirsty soul!

During that same season, I headed off to a local consignment sale, hoping to buy the next season's worth of clothing and shoes for my girls. We were in the middle of raising support for both my husband and me to be on staff with Cru and had taken minimal paychecks to keep our budget in a healthy place. In my mind, I urgently needed to find the items at reduced prices to stretch our clothing budget to cover both of our daughters. Of special importance were shoes for the girls. (How is it that little feet require such huge price tags?) On my way out the door that day, I remember saying a little prayer: "Jesus, You know our needs, our desires, and our budget. Would You please help me find what we need at this sale?"

Walking into the high school gym, I made a beeline for the shoe table. I could not believe my eyes, as they were drawn to a box of pink (*the* favorite color) Stride Rite shoes in my daughter's size. They were brand-new, still in the box, and had a price tag of only $9. Then, as I made my way to the smaller sizes for my youngest daughter, I found another pair of terribly cute, *new* Stride Rite shoes in her size!

I almost started crying right there at the shoe table! It wasn't about the shoes or even the money that I saved (although that was certainly helpful). In that moment, I felt seen by the God of the universe. He was so intimately involved in my life, He provided me with the *exact* items I needed to take care of my children. Never before had two pairs of shoes caused me to give so much worship to God!

The truth is, God sees me. He knows me. He is gentle with me. And that makes all the difference in the world. So wherever you are, Mama, and whatever your story is right now, He sees you and knows you, too. He doesn't see you with disdain or displeasure. He doesn't see you as ineffective because you are busy caring for your children. He sees you with love and affection, and He is there to lead you in your efforts to serve Him and your loved ones.

—SARAH JOHNSON, INDIANAPOLIS, INDIANA

Upside-Down Map

"I had the map, and this was my adventure!"

A road-trip family vacation was underway, and as a determined young mother, I wanted this to be a fun experience for our eight-year-old son—because let's face it, road trips with young children aren't known to be fun!

After perusing books and magazines for ideas (this was in the day before the Internet), I had a Mary Poppins type of bag full of goodies. I had packed an arsenal of special snacks, games, and activities to keep our son occupied. Mind you, this was way before handheld games or DVDs in the headrest!

I made some activities by hand, and I found some at the discount store. My activity lineup had taken me lots of time to prepare, plot, and plan. Based on the length of the day's journey, I had envelopes for him to open introducing each activity. The chosen entertainment could either take five minutes or a full hour, and the anticipation of it was part of the fun! My husband even got involved in the suspense, helping my son track the time until the next unveiling.

Our travels that summer took us through the hills of Arkansas to see extended family. It was a habit of mine to jump off the beaten path and forge a new direction. My motto was "Why drive the boring interstate when you can wind through the countryside and discover new sites?"

During our trip, we passed through small towns, stopped at little mom-and-pop stores, and had picnics with food from local delis at quaint little parks. My selections for car travel entertainment satisfied our son, and we had a memorable time. But, ultimately, he was glad to reach the cousins' house, where he could play with other kids, run and stretch his legs, and talk to people besides grown-ups.

On the return trip, I had another set of fun and games ready. We were about two hours into the trip when the next opened envelope revealed, "Go for a hike." I had planned for us to stop at an Arkansas state park to eat at a cafe and go on an easy, one-mile hike. I had hoped that after a filling lunch and burst of exercise, our son would be tired enough for a long nap. After all, we'd planned our trip home to be a straight drive with no overnight stops.

Grabbing a handy trail map and considering the possibilities, I chose a short, half-mile loop. With excitement, I told my little merry band that we were off for an adventure. I can still remember my son's response: "Oh no! Mom and her adventures!"

Because our trip was in the fall, we had the trail to ourselves, and it was glorious! The leaves were vibrant yellow, red, and gold, unlike the brown foliage of our home state of Texas. The trail went in a downward slope, and we came to a bridge over a river when my husband asked, "Isn't this a little long for a half-mile hike?"

Honestly, I hadn't thought about the time. I looked at the map. There wasn't a marker of any type except for the river. But the half-mile loop didn't have a river, a stream, or even a creek on the map! I looked at the map again. Then I rotated it around.

"Well, the little half-mile trail was to the left, but I accidentally took us to the right. Oops! Looks like we are on a real adventure!"

That was the year I took my little family on a hike with an upside-down map. Yep. I'd read the map wrong and started us off on a three-mile hike through a valley. And of course, we all know that what goes down must come up, right? And come up we did! But first, we took a family vote. Should we retrace our steps, unsure of how far we'd already hiked? Or, should we forge ahead and stay on the trail, hoping for only three miles? I don't remember whether the vote was unanimous, but we decided to go forward because I had the map and this was my adventure! At one point, my husband looked over his shoulder and said, "It says here there is also a five-mile hike. You didn't take us on the five-mile hike, did you?"

"No!" I answered, with a strong voice, trying to convince myself of my overconfident answer. (I hoped and prayed I was right.) Judging by the sun filtering through the trees and the direction the five-mile trail took, I was fairly confident I had my bearings. And with lots of time to think during that hike, I was reminded of Psalm 32:8 in which the Lord says, "I will guide you along the best pathway for your life. I will advise you and watch over you" (NLT).

We were literally trusting God to help us find the best pathway back to our car. And eventually, the sights began to look familiar. Then we heard some sounds. As we hushed and strained our ears, we heard voices up ahead. We were still down in the valley and the parking lot was up above us. Even though we were on a well-maintained trail, I heaved a sigh of relief at hearing those faint voices.

When we broke through the tree line onto the pavement and saw our car in the parking lot, we let out a whoop and a holler. We heaved a sigh of relief at seeing civilization. My planned twenty-minute hike had ballooned to two hours! All three of us were winded, thirsty, and ready to rest. And we still had a six-hour drive ahead of us. Somehow, we made it home that night, albeit two or three hours behind schedule. Now when someone asks, "Have you ever vacationed in the Ouachita Mountains?" I always reply, "Yes! That's the vacation when I got us lost because I followed an upside-down map!"

For all you moms out there who sometimes misguide your families on hiking trails or other adventures in life, don't panic. You have a God who loves you and will faithfully guide you through every valley—no upside-down maps included!

—KIM STEADMAN, GRAND PRAIRIE, TEXAS

Carefree or in Control?

"My son's toddler-ness—
his being unpredictable and demanding—
had left me feeling out of control."

Before I became a mom, I had a picture in my head of the type of mother I would be. I would schedule everything out—the feedings, bath times, and playtimes—all with classical music playing in the background. I would cook and clean while the baby was sleeping or playing peacefully. I would go to Mommy-and-Me classes, and my son would always be doing something intentional, artistic, or educational. Of course, in my mind, I thought I would handle uncertain and new circumstances with ease. I would find joy in the unexpected and laugh when my baby spilled something. After all, that would be an opportunity for creativity! When I thought of my future self, I felt laid-back. I kept thinking, *How hard can motherhood be?* I was wrong—so, so wrong.

The truth is, I do much better with boundaries and schedules, so it came as a complete shock when I found myself struggling to get my bearings those first few months—and dare I say, first few *years* of motherhood. While natural patterns emerged as I followed my son's leading, it was hard to be consistent. Once I had a routine down, my son would outgrow it and move on to another pattern. Or, he would get sick and want to be held all night, which would throw the next day's plans completely off. And when schedules didn't stick, I grew frustrated. After all, I'm not what you would call the "carefree" type. I need structure and organization, but I secretly admire moms who let their kids throw around paint and splash in puddles. I don't know why I thought my personality would suddenly change after I gave birth!

Around my son's second birthday, my husband and I talked about what disciplining our son would look like. After all, he was older and we felt like he understood more. I mentioned how we should try our best to discipline out of love and not anger. We would need to display self-control when he was acting out of control. We would explain *why* we were disciplining. However, that same day, I found myself already worn out by midmorning. During my son's morning snack, I told him no a little more harshly than I had intended when he threw his food on the floor for what felt like the hundredth time. He had also banged his head against his chair in order to get a reaction out of me and slapped me when I got close to him. When I looked at him, he smiled. My frustration reached a breaking point, and I did not handle things in the controlled manner we'd discussed. After my son finished eating, I took him to the bathroom to wash up. That's when my husband gently reminded me of the talk we'd had only an hour earlier. I grew quiet. My son's toddler-ness—his being unpredictable and demanding—had left me feeling out of control.

Later that afternoon, we took our son outside to play. Since our toddler has low muscle tone, his fine motor skills are delayed, which means that while he is walking, he still needs a lot of supervision. While I want to be the mom who lets her son run around and not be fearful of falls, I'm always a bit more cautious. We stay on the grass on purpose. Not only is it softer than concrete, but it also takes more effort for him to step since his feet sink in. He is learning to shift his weight and balance. I know this is good for him, but I look at his feet and how he moves and wonder if it's too much sometimes. I don't want him to fall improperly and twist his ankles or, worse, fall on his face. While we were in the front yard, a neighbor drove by and watched as my husband and I walked and played with our son. It must have been a funny scene as I kept running in front of my son to make sure he didn't fall. Again, it was all about control. My initial thoughts of being a carefree mom had turned into endless moments of fighting to maintain control.

It wasn't until I began to think about God, our perfect parent, that I realized my struggle for control wasn't necessary. After all, God is fully in control of the whole universe and our lives! He knows how to discipline with grace and love. He sees us and knows how frail we are, but He knows when to hold us tight and when to let us go. He teaches us through the difficulties in life to build our faith muscles. God sees us in our shortcomings and loves us anyway.

Psalm 84:11 says this: "For the LORD God is a sun and shield; the LORD will give grace and glory; no good thing will He withhold from those who walk uprightly" (NKJV).

The Lord knows we are not perfect. Even when we try to fake it or pretend to be someone else, He sees through it all. He knows our tendencies and His perfect love covers our sins. While it's easy for us to want to be someone we're not or wish that we were a different type of mom, each of us is the perfect mother for our children. In the same way that God chose you, He chose your child for you, and He knows that in every way, you are exactly what your child needs today.

Whether you thrive on fixed schedules or enjoy handling life as it comes, you are worthy of motherhood. And if you feel that you need to be in control because you are afraid (like me), remember that God is with you. He is there to forgive you when you've made a mistake, and He is there to catch you when you fall.

—JANNET YOO, CERRITOS, CALIFORNIA

You Are Mine

*"There isn't a mother on earth
who doesn't know that 'look'
on their child's face."*

After my husband's grandmother passed away, we inherited her solid-oak dining room set. Grammie had been proud of it, and every time we visited her, she adorned it with beautiful table runners, vases, and seasonal decorations. The beloved table was a good representation of her life—strong, steady, and resolute in purpose.

As we made that three-hour drive home from Cape Cod, with Grammie's dining room set wedged between our kids (ages five and ten), I thought about the legacy and heritage we were bringing home. My husband had sat at that table for almost every major holiday and birthday of his childhood, just as his dad had done before him. Grammie's dining room table had hosted friends for tea, grandchildren for ice cream sundaes, and countless meals for ordinary days.

However, because of the way our home is designed, we didn't have space to give Grammie's dining room set its full pomp and circumstance the way it had been displayed in her house. Instead of using it for formal dining, we decided to use it as our everyday kitchen table. We knew that Grammie would be thrilled to know her table was being put to good use!

When we got home and set up the table and chairs in our kitchen, we marveled at how it fit just right. We thanked

God for the beautiful life that Grammie lived, and then I gave the children a very stern warning: "This isn't just an ordinary table," I began. "This is Grammie's table. It's special to us because it was in her home. This is the table that Daddy sat at when he was a little boy. And now we get to use it too."

My ten-year-old son didn't care for this lecture, and frankly, it wasn't aimed at him. It was for my five-year-old daughter, Lola, who loves art, creating things, and making messes involving glue and glitter.

I continued, "We all need to do our part to keep it beautiful. We can't color with markers or paint at this table; you'll need to use your desk for art projects now. Someday, Lola, this dining room set will be yours. That is part of the reason why Grammie gave it to us; she wanted you to have it someday. When you get married, you can take it with you to the home you start with your husband."

Everyone left the conversation on the same page, knowing the table was special and that we were going to treat it kindly. I patted myself on the back for setting expectations and boundaries.

For the first six months, it was smooth sailing with Grammie's table. We moved my daughter's art projects to her desk or to a table out on the deck. However, one afternoon I walked into the kitchen and knew something was wrong. My sweet daughter had that "look" on her face. There isn't a mother on earth who doesn't know that "look" on their child's face. It's the one that tells you your child has been up to no good and is trying to figure out how to sneak it past you.

As I walked closer to the table, I could see that her napkin was in an odd place, as if she was hiding something underneath it. I wasn't sure what to expect when I picked up the napkin, but I certainly was not prepared for what I saw. My daughter had carved out LOLA deep into the oak table with the prong of a fork. A thousand questions came flying out of my mouth. My words were sharp and my tone was clipped.

"What were you thinking? Why would you do this? This is Grammie's special table! These marks are DEEP! Why did you think this was a good idea? Mommy can clean a lot of things, but this is NOT ONE OF THEM! I don't even think this can be fixed. Grammie's table will always have your name on it now!"

On and on I scolded as her eyes welled up with tears. She knew she had made a big mistake. Almost immediately I regretted my harshness. As I calmed myself down, my daughter took a deep breath and with a quivering voice said, "But, Mama, you said that the table was mine. I used my fork to write my name on it to show that it is mine. I'm sorry that I didn't make a good choice. But now that my name is written on it, we'll all know who it belongs to."

As she finished her defense, I felt the Holy Spirit whisper to me, "You are Mine. Just like Lola has written her name on Grammie's table, I have written My name on your heart. You are Mine. You can't erase it, clean it, or take it back. I have called you and claimed you. My love for you is unable to be revoked. You are Mine."

My posture toward my daughter softened, and I was overwhelmed with the love God has for His children. I scooped her up in my arms and started to cry, too. "Lola, this wasn't a good choice, but it is just a table. I am sorry for the way I reacted."

That day, I remembered the words in Isaiah 43:1: "But now, this is what the LORD says—He who created you,

Jacob, He who formed you, Israel: 'Do not fear, for I have redeemed you; I have summoned you by name; you are Mine'" (NIV).

For every mama reading this and who needs a reminder of who they are in the Lord, beyond all mistakes and failures, never forget that You are His. He has created you and redeemed you. He knows you by name.

My daughter is a bit older now, and her name is still carved on Grammie's table. As it turns out, it could have been repaired with putty and shellac. But every time I see it, I hear the Holy Spirit whisper one word to me: *Mine*. The name stays.

—NJ RONGNER, HOLYOKE, MASSACHUSETTS

A Little More Time

*"In my hurriedness,
I had made things more complicated
and caused my frustration to grow."*

I am a list maker and schedule keeper, which doesn't always coincide with being a fun mom. So in order to get my to-do list done with my girls in tow, I've often disguised errands as fun outings.

One day, I had my daughters, Adrian and Hayley, and their little friend Anna with me as I made various stops to finish the never-ending to-do list. The girls were entertaining themselves by telling silly jokes and enjoying being together. However, I was tired. It had been a long week. Each time we stopped, I felt like I was running a marathon to unlock three car seats and wait (somewhat) patiently for them to climb out of the car. Of course, they were unaware of my schedule and list of errands.

With my last errand needing to be accomplished at the mall, I enticed the girls with a treat if they would "please move a little bit faster." They squealed with delight and made it their mission to help me get my errands completed.

However, by the time we made it to the mall, I was *done*. As we pulled into the parking spot, I glanced at the clock and realized dinnertime was fast approaching. I had promised them a treat right before dinner—what was I thinking? But a promise is a promise, and I couldn't disappoint the girls, who had been so good. So, I climbed out of the car (one more time), unbuckled them, and waited impatiently for them to exit the car. The girls were oblivious to my struggle as their minds were filled with the promise of a yummy treat. Once my errand was finished, I tried to encourage them to choose a treat that was easy and quick—like a small lollipop. But they *all* wanted Orange Julius. The only thing that made me feel better was that the ingredients included orange juice. So, I purchased their drinks and we headed back to the car.

It took a bit of effort, but finally all three girls were in their car seats with their drinks properly placed in their cup holders. I took a deep breath. *We did it!* Then I put the key in the ignition and turned it. Nothing. The engine sounded like it was going to start but didn't. I tried again and again. Finally, I stopped turning the key. Being a mom who believes in prayer and wants my girls to know the power of God over every situation, I paused and prayed out loud with six little ears listening behind me.

When I finished praying, I looked in the rearview mirror and saw their little faces looking at me expectantly. What was going to happen? I slowly turned the key thinking, "Okay, God, this would be a great time to show these little girls how You answer prayer." But instead, the turn of the key produced nothing. I looked at the clock and realized my friend would soon be arriving at my house to pick up her daughter. Quickly, I jumped out of the car and unbuckled the girls to run back into the mall (as fast as you can run with three little girls sipping Orange Julius drinks). I needed to find a pay phone since this occurred before the convenience of cell phones.

Once I found the phone at the other end of the mall, I realized I didn't have enough change. I quickly walked to another store and made a small purchase to get some cash back. What an ordeal to just make a phone call. Then, I ran back to the phone with three little girls tagging behind me, their Orange Julius drinks spilling down their fronts.

As I put my money into the pay phone, I prayed my husband would answer. When he picked up, I was so relieved to hear his voice! By this time, I was frustrated, tired, and feeling guilty that this "fun" errand time was turning into a nightmare. I told him that the car wouldn't start. He went through a list of things I should try when I interrupted him, saying, "Please just come and get us. The girls are tired, my friend is coming, and it is dinnertime." He could tell I was at the end of my rope and said he would get there as soon as possible. I hung up the phone and told the girls that Daddy was coming to get us. For the final time that day, I put all three girls in their car seats, thankful it wasn't hot outside, and sat down in my seat to wait. Wow, what a day!

As I sat there, I thought I might as well try starting the motor one more time. I put the key in the ignition and turned it. The car started! I couldn't believe it. As I sat there dumbfounded, a small voice in the back of the car said quietly, "Maybe we should have given Jesus a little more time."

I couldn't help but laugh. I said, "You know, Anna, you are right!" My daughters' little friend taught me a great lesson that day. I prayed but didn't give Jesus a lot of time to answer my prayer. In my hurriedness, I had made things more complicated and caused my frustration to grow.

If only I had given Jesus a little more time.

That phrase now stays with me as I journey through life. To give Jesus a little more time, to wait on Him when life seems overwhelming, and to trust Him when I don't understand. That is always the best decision. As a mom and now a nana, I have found that I'm not alone as I learn to wait on Him. For moms who are rushing through life, this Scripture is a great reminder to slow down and give Jesus more time: "But those who wait on the LORD shall renew their strength; they shall mount up with wings like eagles, they shall run and not be weary, they shall walk and not faint" (ISAIAH 40:31 NKJV).

—DEBBIE COLE, DUVALL, WASHINGTON

Maybe Later

*"I had ignored my daughter—not in the sense that
I wasn't taking care of her and doing what needed to
be done, but in the sense that she needed me to give her
my full attention and take interest in what she was doing."*

As a wife and stay-at-home mom, juggling has become a normal part of my routine. One of my juggles is to wake up earlier than everyone else in the house so that I can have a little time to myself. During those quiet moments, I read my Bible and work out to set the tone for the day. I've grown accustomed to wearing different hats as part of the norm. After all, many hats are required, as I'm a "momager" (a mom who manages children), a blogger, a podcaster, and a travel agent.

On one of those juggling days when I'd been busy cleaning the house, my seven-year-old daughter asked, "Mommy, can we play?" I told her I was busy. Again at dinnertime, when I was running behind schedule, my daughter asked, "Mommy can you play with me?" I told her I was preparing dinner. After dinner, I asked the kids to go downstairs to play in the basement. And just as I sat down for a much-needed break, my daughter asked again, "Mommy, can we play before I go downstairs?"

I felt as though I was on autopilot when I said, "Tahlia, honey, I worked so hard today and I am *really* tired. Mommy just needs a little break, okay? Why don't you go on downstairs and we will play later."

I sat down to relax on the couch, only to have my son

stomp up the stairs completely annoyed. Wearily, I asked what was wrong. He informed me that Tahlia was downstairs crying. Come to find out, he had written on her book and she was upset about it. I called for my daughter and asked to see the book. The mark was so tiny, it was hardly a mark at all! Even though her brother apologized, she kept crying. It was then that I realized something deeper was going on.

"Tahlia," I said, looking her in the eyes. "Is something else wrong?"

As tears rolled down her face, she nodded her head. She admitted feeling like everyone was ignoring her. *Oh boy,* I thought. *I know where this conversation is going.* However, I gave her the opportunity to express her feelings and asked, "Sweetie, why do you feel ignored?" She mentioned how her brother was always hanging out with his friends, but then she got to the heart of the matter by saying, "And you are always too busy to play with me."

That was it.

I had ignored my daughter—not in the sense that I wasn't taking care of her and doing what needed to be done, but in the sense that she needed me to give her my full attention and take interest in what she was doing. Wow. I was humbled.

As a mom who always tries to make sure things around the house run smoothly, it's hard to hear that your child is dissatisfied with what you are doing (or not doing). I felt terrible. How could I make sure the house was taken care of *and* play with my kids at the same time? I looked at her and apologized for my behavior. After all, kids are little people too!

I pulled her close and told her that I was trying my best to make sure everyone was comfortable and cared for. I told her that because I had so much to do, I didn't always have time to play. That's when she looked back at me and said, "I understand, Mommy." (Oh, my heart!)

In that moment, I realized that balance is the key. Time spent with my kids is more important than making sure my house looks perfect. It reminds me of Proverbs 22:6: "Train up a child in the way he should go, and when he is old he will not depart from it" (NKJV). If my children see that I am putting cleaning before their needs, then I am training them to believe that practical things come before spiritual things and to-do lists come before relationships.

As moms, we want things to be right. We want things to be in order. But in our quest to make sure dinner is cooked, clothes are washed, and the house is clean, we must keep in mind what is most important—our relationships. The thing is, God will not be upset with us for putting laundry aside in order to take a walk in the park with our kids. We need to learn to extend grace and patience to ourselves, just as we strive to extend grace and patience to our children. We set the tone as adults, so we have to be mindful of how we behave. Our children are watching us and learning from us.

I also learned through that experience that our words mean everything to our kids. When I told my daughter that I was going to play with her but kept putting her off, I was teaching her to not hold others accountable or be accountable herself. Our children learn from what they see and hear us do. And while I know how difficult it is to leave those dirty dishes in the sink, I also know that time spent with my kids is much more important. The dishes will always be waiting!

God will help you balance your life and your priorities. Just pray and ask Him to give you wisdom throughout the day. And the next time your child asks you to stop and play, turn your "maybe later" into a moment of connection with the little person who is counting on you.

—TAMARA SOUTH, BRONX, NEW YORK

The Superpower of Rest

*"What I wouldn't give for a moment of silence
cuddled up by the fireplace or a nap in the hammock
with a good book."*

I wish I could take a break, I thought for the hundredth time that day. But between checking off tasks from my to-do list and prioritizing what I should do next, I couldn't even think of taking a break. In fact, I silently shamed myself for wanting to relax and kick up my feet with my favorite cup of tea (sigh). But before I could finish beating myself up, I heard someone call my name.

"Mom!"

I immediately thought, *Maybe this time they need me for something important. After all, they can't be starving. I already cooked for them!* But when my son kept calling me, my mind assumed it must be an emergency.

Instantly, the Mama Bear in me kicked in. I rushed to the living room with my imaginary mom-cape fluttering behind me. I came to the rescue, only to be asked if I'd seen his favorite shoes. Of course I had! I'd already picked them up from the middle of the floor!

I went back to my to-do list, wishing again for that relaxing cup of tea. On my way down the hall, I remembered the groceries I needed to pick up and the load of laundry I needed to wash. But before I could even take ten steps, I heard another call.

"Mom!" (This time it was my daughter.)

I snapped around, trying to mask my irritation. She asked if I could take her to a friend's house, even though she already knew the answer. She left the room pouting, while I tried to rein in my previous thoughts. What was I doing before I got interrupted? Oh, right, the laundry. I sat on the edge of the bed, trying to muster the motivation to get moving. I ran my fingers through my hair as if I could capture my thoughts in the palm of my hand. What I wouldn't give for a moment of silence cuddled up by the fireplace or a nap in the hammock with a good book.

By the time I reached for the laundry basket, I heard another voice calling my name. I tried to ignore it, but it grew louder. It asked, *What if I just hide in here for a while. No one will notice if I just take five minutes.* Next, it was the voice of my husband calling for me. What was it *now*? (My inner voice was now yelling in frustration.) I emerged from the closet to meet his frown. Then his brow softened. He could see that I was tired.

"When was the last time you had a break?" he asked, his words covered in concern.

I couldn't answer him. I hadn't allowed myself to take a break in so long, I honestly couldn't remember. I thought taking breaks would mean I was weak or lazy, not fulfilling my duties as a woman. But come to find out, that simply wasn't true.

My husband insisted I take a break—a moment with Jesus—and forget about everything else. I obliged, acting as if I was forced to do it. At first I sat in unease, uncomfortable with rest. But then, my shoulders dropped and the wrinkles in my forehead disappeared, along with all the negative thoughts I'd been thinking. I took a deep breath and exhaled. I whispered to God and His peace surrounded me. I realized how much I'd missed those quiet moments with Him. All the roles and responsibilities drifted away, and I was a little girl in the presence of my Father. I did what most girls do in the security of their dads. I imagined, played, and ate ice cream without worrying about the carbs. Most importantly, I rested.

Of course, within a few hours, the rest came to an end and I went back to reality. But something had changed. I wasn't on edge anymore. I wasn't checking off a mental to-do list. I was at peace. Because I'd stepped away for a time, I was able to be fully present with my family. That's when it hit me. God created rest for us, and when we don't utilize that gift, we don't function as well as we could.

My friends, the guilt and shame we feel for needing rest is a lie we've believed. Somehow, we're convinced that even our self-care routines need to be productive. We fight to be superwomen for others yet push ourselves to the side. But who comes to the rescue if Superwoman loses her powers? We've never been taught that our superpowers come from rest. And in order to properly take care of others, we have to take care of ourselves first. The second of God's greatest commandments says, "Love your neighbor as yourself" (MARK 12:31 NIV). We're good at the "loving your neighbor" part, but we often forget the "as yourself" part.

When we are too busy with lofty lists and goals, we forget to take moments to connect our spirits with God's Spirit. But that's where we find rest. And rest is required for our assignments as women.

The bottom line is, it's okay to take a break! You won't be condemned for soaking in the tub with bubbles and candles for an hour. The world won't end if you get ice cream by yourself or take a long drive and listen to your favorite music. Your family will survive if you take an afternoon break at the beach. But *you* won't survive if you keep neglecting yourself.

Think about it this way: When your children are restless, you lull them to sleep. When your husband is hungry, you give him something to eat. When the dog needs to go for a walk, you take him. But you neglect giving yourself a break when you need it because of a self-imposed pressure to do it all. My friends, that's not fair to *you*. Listen to the Holy Spirit when He gives you the gentle nudge to rest. When you find yourself snappy with your children, find a quiet place. When you find yourself at odds with your husband for no reason, take a moment. Build into your schedule time for yourself the same way you schedule everything else. It's okay.

Let's remember God's greatest commandments—not only the one about loving our neighbors, but the second part as well. It's okay to take that five-minute break, read that book, or go for that run. In fact, your family will feel more loved because you're loving them as you love yourself.

—ERICA GLENN, GRAND RAPIDS, MICHIGAN

What's Really Needed

*"In my moment of parental paralysis
a very gentle internal voice whispered,
'Is tonight about what you wanted
or what your family needed?'"*

One of my favorite verses in the Bible is Psalm 16:11: "You will show me the way of life, granting me the joy of Your presence and the pleasures of living with You forever" (NLT).

On this journey of life, I get directionally challenged sometimes. Life can twist and turn and leave me confused. But when I take time to be with my Father, I find myself joy-filled and full of direction. So no matter what my age, I always want to view myself as a child of God and rely on Him to guide me.

It's similar to how my kids look to me for direction. They ask me the "why and how" of doing things (except when they know how to do it all by themselves). They seek me out and want me to be fully present when I'm with them. They find joy in my presence! However, sometimes I complicate this. I don't stand still long enough to give them my full attention. I'm not always available to look them in the eye, give them a hug, or say a quick prayer for them. Sometimes, I overlook what's really needed and continue to do things my way.

When our oldest daughter, Ava, was two, I learned a big lesson about what's most important. Ava had an intensity about her that set her apart. On one hand, she could be super affectionate, but on the other hand, her big brown eyes could stare a hole right through you! That same intensity had a way of throwing me off as a mom, and many times I simply didn't know what to do with her reactions.

One night in particular, my husband and I were preparing for a week-long trip. It wasn't a suitable trip for small kids, so we had decided to leave Ava with family. On this picturesque night, we decided to make the most of our time with Ava since we would be separated for a week. We chose one of our favorite restaurants with ambient lighting, soft jazzy music, tables full of people, and the hustle and bustle of servers weaving in and out of tables. The restaurant was a big open dining area, and we were seated smack-dab in the middle of it all! Now, if you like a lively dinner party, that was the place to be. But it didn't take long for us to realize Ava was not enjoying it at all.

I could see the intensity in her eyes growing. Her brow began to furrow. Her lips started to stiffen, and her body was tense. I knew what was coming next—*the cry*. It was the howl that would pierce your ears and drown out all conversation. It was the kind of wailing that would turn all eyes on you—like it or not!

I didn't like her behavior at all. Her little tantrum was ruining my picturesque family night. It was definitely not what I had in mind for our quality time together. I tried to calm Ava down while my husband tried to get our food ordered. We realized rather quickly that our hourglass had turned into a countdown timer and was flashing bright red!

We finally got the food ordered, but her crying had turned into an all-out meltdown. Quite literally, Ava had melted out of my lap into a pool of tears under the table. In my two years of parenting her, I had never experienced this before. I found myself battling a mix of emotions. I was embarrassed, angry, *hungry*, and confused. And I was parentally paralyzed. My thoughts ran rampant as I asked myself, Do I get under the table and talk to her eyeball-to-eyeball? Do I pull her back up here on my lap and hold her until this is over? Should I take her to the bathroom and discipline her?

If you've ever had a moment like that, you know the whole gamut of thoughts going through your mind. But perhaps like me, your body couldn't move and your mouth stayed quiet. In my moment of parental paralysis a very gentle internal voice whispered, "Is tonight about what you wanted or what your family *needed*?" Ugh! I realized that in my effort to create a special moment, I hadn't considered who I was creating it for. Was it for me or was it for *us*?

I realized that what my two-year-old really wanted was *me*. She didn't want or need the ambient lighting, background music, or to be waited on hand-and-foot by our oh-so-patient server.

She would have been happy with a bag of crackers on our living room floor with her daddy and me playing with her.

Our Ava is thirteen years old now, and I can honestly say that the dramatic meltdown and the still, small voice became a pivotal point for me. I learned so much about myself, my parenting style, and my oldest daughter—all in a matter of thirty minutes.

I learned that I could be in the same place with my family but not actually be present. I also learned that I needed to be a student of my children—to study how they respond to certain things. Once I learned how my children thrive, I could parent more effectively.

As I read my favorite verse again, I'm reminded of the importance of simply being in the presence of God and each other. "You will show me the way of life, granting me the joy of Your presence and the pleasures of living with You forever" (PSALM 16:11 NLT).

It's not about forcing moments together. It's about creating moments that meet the needs of one another. It means cultivating flexibility all around. But when everyone's needs are met, a greater sense of stability develops.

Even though we had to get our food to go that night, I walked out of the restaurant feeling confident that I was doing what was *needed*. And that was far better than what I'd originally wanted for myself.

—HANNAH BECHTEL, SOUTH JORDAN, UTAH

Grace When We Forget

*"My heart sank into my stomach
as my husband rushed out the door
to retrieve our four-year-old son.
I sat there in disbelief.
I had so many emotions raging,
from fear to astonishment."*

It was an early Sunday morning, and I was up enjoying my coffee while sitting peacefully in the stillness of the room. I wanted to spend some time with God and gather my thoughts before the busy morning began. With two young children, I hadn't found the time to enjoy my relationship with the Lord like I had before kids. When our firstborn daughter, Katie, came along, I struggled to find regular time to read the Bible and pray. But when our son, Matthew, was born, I found it extra difficult to carve out quiet time with the Lord. What a big adjustment it was for me to go from parenting one child to two!

But there I was that Sunday morning, taking in the sweet sound of nothingness before the mad rush of getting ready for church. Sundays were always a bit hectic as I made breakfast, pressed clothes for my husband, and helped my kids get ready and out the door. Katie was six years old at the time and reminded me daily that she was a "big girl" and didn't need my help. Of course, this just made me laugh as I remembered my early childhood days when I had said the same thing to my mama. I guess it's universal how we women are so independent and strong-willed. At least that's true for me!

But now, at the age of fifty-six, I miss my mama with all my heart and wish for just a few moments to sit with her and see her smile again. I would love to hear her voice, to glean some wisdom, and to ask how she raised five children without losing her mind. Often, I find myself whispering a prayer to God for a good day—a day of remembering all the things I need to do—especially since I'm becoming so forgetful lately. (Just another sign of life's marathon!)

Back to that Sunday morning, I finished my quiet time with God and served my family a quick breakfast. Things were going great until I happened to notice the time. The church service started in ten minutes! In a mad rush, my husband, Robert, jumped in his car and went ahead of me. I ran to the back room to get myself and my daughter ready. In record time, we were dressed, groomed, and ready to go. I grabbed Katie and off we went! We walked into the church with only seconds to spare. And as we sat down next to Robert, I let out a deep breath.

"Where is Matthew?" I inquired, not seeing my son in the seat next to him. My husband looked at me, puzzled.

"What do you mean?" he asked, looking concerned. "I thought you were bringing him."

To our complete horror, we realized that Matthew was not with us at church! My heart sank into my stomach as my husband rushed out the door to retrieve our four-year-old son. I sat there in disbelief. I had so many emotions raging, from fear to astonishment. I was literally dumbfounded that we actually forgot our son at home!

It seemed like an eternity before Robert (with Matthew close behind) walked into the service. To my surprise, my son had the biggest smile on his face. I reached over and whispered, "Oh my goodness, Matthew, are you okay?"

Excitedly, he went on to tell me about his great adventure at home alone. He said he didn't know where anyone was, so he decided to go out back and jump on the trampoline. A few neighbor kids joined him, and they were having a blast! They were still jumping and playing when Robert showed up. As he was sharing his adventure, my heart kept repeating, *Thank You, God. Thank You that my son is okay.* All through the church service, I pondered the different outcomes of leaving Matthew at home. Over and over, I thanked the Lord and asked for His forgiveness.

After all, how could I have forgotten my own son?

There is no doubt that this experience was a defining moment for me. That day, I realized some pretty significant truths about God and about myself . I realized how thankful I am that our heavenly Father's eyes are always on us. As it states in Psalm 139:1–4, "O Lord, You have searched me and known me. You know my sitting down and my rising up; You understand my thought afar off. You comprehend my path and my lying down, and are acquainted with all my ways. For there is not a word on my tongue, but behold, O Lord, You know it altogether" (NKJV).

What a personal, present God we serve! I find this so reassuring, especially in times when life gets busy and overwhelming. He keeps His eyes on us and our children— even four-year-olds who get left home alone! Even when we miss the mark, forget the big things, the small things, and everything in between, our God never does. He is always there to watch over us and bring us back to where we need to be.

Moms, I hope and pray that you will find great comfort

in the promises of God. Isaiah 49:15–16 says, "Can a mother forget the infant at her breast, walk away from the baby she bore? But even if mothers forget, I'd never forget you—never. Look, I've written your names on the backs of My hands" (THE MESSAGE).

If our names are written on God's hands, He isn't going to forget about us. He isn't going to be too distracted to watch over us. What a comforting thought! He grants mercy when we mess up. He offers forgiveness without partiality, and He gives us grace when we forget.

—NANCY LINCOLN, DEWITT, IOWA

Promises, Promises

*"With my family finally asleep, I climbed into my spot
and listened to the beautiful breathing
of a sleeping choir in different rhythms—so sweet.
These were my closest little friends and
the love of my life. Tears rolled down my cheeks
as my heart whispered, 'I love You, Jesus.'"*

Have you ever made a promise to your kids—like, a *big* promise? Perhaps you promised a trip, an event, or a costly item, but right before it was time to fulfill it, something came along to derail your plans. For our family, the big promise had always been a trip to Disney World. We planned to take that trip one day but didn't know when or if it would ever happen.

Then one year, we found ourselves on a last-minute trip to Florida to pick up our long-awaited goldendoodle. When we checked the map, we saw that our new puppy was in a town not too far from our favorite beach, so we decided to leave a week early and enjoy a little vacation.

However, with no hotel reservation, we ended up driving in the middle of the night without finding a single vacancy! We searched all the hotels in the area that met our criteria: two rooms and under $300. But we found nothing. We even drove to a hotel that said they had rooms available but found out once we arrived the rooms *weren't* available after all. As I walked away from the check-in desk, I could sense the Holy Spirit nudging me to move on. We can *do this*, I thought.

After all, we have a fifteen-passenger Sprinter van!

Walking across the parking lot, I approached our van window with a smile—a smile that only a spouse who's been driving for twenty hours understands. My husband, Scott, gave me the "No, babe, we are *not* sleeping in the van" look. I smiled back. "We can *sooo* do this! It's going to be fun!" I announced.

We parked under a palm tree and woke the kids to tell them. Of course, they were expecting a cool room, a hot shower, comfy beds, and a hot breakfast in the morning. So when I excitedly announced we were going to sleep in the van, I quickly added that we would head to Walmart early in the morning and get snacks for breakfast on the beach. That did the trick. I was excited and so were they. It would be an adventure!

After using the hotel restrooms, we spread all the bags over the parking lot and dug for pajamas, blankets, and pillows. An hour later, my husband settled on the back seat, my eighteen-year-old son on the next seat, and my fourteen-year-old on the seat in front of that. The babies were placed on my yoga mats, while my seventeen- and sixteen-year-old girls piled into the driver and passenger seats. I claimed my spot on the front bench. With my family finally asleep, I climbed into my spot and listened to the beautiful breathing of a sleeping choir in different rhythms—so sweet. These were my closest little friends and the love of my life. Tears rolled down my cheeks as my heart whispered, "I love You, Jesus."

However, after three days of sun and sand and no showers to rinse us off, we were a stinky bunch! We still couldn't find any vacant rooms in any hotel along the beach. With two days left until we could pick up our new puppy, we made a new, exciting decision. This was the moment—our *big* promise was suddenly doable. Scott and I pulled over and asked the kids to stay in the van so we could "talk."

"You know, there are rooms available in Orlando and it's not that far," I said.

"You wanna go for it?" my husband replied, excitedly. "You wanna surprise the kids with a day at Disney World before we get the puppy?"

Bubbling over inside, I couldn't wait to tell the kids. After all, they had not complained or grumbled once during our three-day adventure. In fact, there had been a new level of rest in the Lord and a sweet closeness as a family. We called a family meeting.

"Kids, please step out of the van for a minute and get in a circle. We want to have a family discussion," I said, trying to hide my excitement.

After a few seconds of silence, my husband announced, "Kids, Mommy and I have decided we are getting a hotel in Orlando and we're going to the Magic Kingdom for a day."

There was silence, followed by jumping and excitement. Happy tears flowed. One child kept staring at us with big, tear-filled eyes, repeating, "Really, Mommy and Daddy? Are we really going to Disney World?" It was an incredible week for all of us. We set out to get a dog, slept in the van for three days, ended up with a surprise Disney day, and finished our trip with our new puppy in tow!

If you as a mommy have ever wanted to promise something to your children but the time, money, and resources weren't there, please know you aren't alone. We all want to give our children the best of memories, but often it feels like there are obstacles at every turn. And sometimes we are surprised with a gift we never saw coming! Our attitude of gratefulness in those moments is important as we model for our kids a heart that is thankful to our heavenly Father for *all* He provides for us—for taking care of our daily needs and for surprising us with unexpected bonus gifts.

First Thessalonians 5:18 says, "In everything give thanks; for this is the will of God in Christ Jesus for you" (NKJV). God wants us to depend on Him and thank Him in *every* situation—when things go as planned and when they don't; when we feel confident about our next steps and when we're filled with uncertainty. God has promised He will take care of us.

I pray that each of us will be able to surrender all our plans (and promises) to God and know that He will provide for our families. Things might not turn out the way we expect, but oftentimes it's better than we ever could have imagined!

—JENN HARBOUR, TYLER, TEXAS

Stuff Happens

*"In a crazy spiral of 'baby brain,' I lost my mind.
At least that's the only explanation I have
for what came next—I took my toddler out of the cart."*

I was frantically trying to run a few errands before I had to pick up my oldest child from preschool. Utmost in my mind was this pressing question: *How much can I check off my to-do list before I have to make the mad dash back to school (and not be the last mommy to pick up)?*

To add to the chaos, I had my squirmy toddler in the grocery cart and "a bun in the oven." At eight months pregnant, I felt enormous and slow. Add to the mix uncomfortable and harried, and you have a pretty good idea of how I was feeling that day. I was trying to do too much in too little time—and it was only going to get worse.

I waddled up and down the aisles of the grocery store, trying to wrestle the aforementioned toddler back into his seat. He definitely *did not* want to cooperate. And who could blame him? I was thoroughly distracted, throwing this and that into the cart, trying to bribe him with animal crackers, and moving as fast as I could. It was not a fun time for mommy or child.

And my stupid purse! It kept falling off my arm, so I tossed it in the cart next to my toddler, who promptly threw it on the floor. I suppose I could have worn a fanny pack to keep my arms free, but I'm not sure they come in the girth I needed at eight months pregnant. And any stylish bag with long straps is impractical for a mom of three kids who needed to stash juice boxes, gummy bears, and basically half the house in it. Besides, if I'd had one of those stylish purses, it probably would have strangled me with all my bending, twisting, and turning.

I needed my hands free to grab groceries and keep my toddler from lurching out of the cart. In desperation, I decided to bury my purse beneath the growing mound of groceries in my cart. I pawed my way past the frozen waffles and boxes of cereal to the bottom of the cart and planted my purse there. Then I covered it with piles of fruit snacks, granola bars, and juice boxes and set my toddler as guard. Who would dare brave such a formidable foe?

We continued through the store as fast as I could waddle with preschool pick-up time fast approaching. However, the faster I tried to move, the squirmier my toddler became. And in a crazy spiral of "baby brain," I lost my mind. At least that's the only explanation I have for what came next—I took my toddler out of the cart.

Of course, he didn't stay obediently next to the cart or securely hold on to the edge of my shirt. He didn't walk silently beside me as I finished my frantic shopping. He immediately bolted around the corner. And I, slow and huge, chased him. Three minutes later, I cornered him and strapped his screaming little self back in the cart.

Finally, I made it to the checkout line and began swiftly unloading my items onto the conveyor belt. I got through item after item, right down to the bottom of the cart.

Then it happened. The cashier sweetly inquired, "How would you like to pay today—cash or credit?" I looked down at my empty cart as the horrible realization hit. My purse, with both my credit cards and my cash, was gone! In the three minutes I had been chasing my toddler, someone had walked up to my cart, plunged his or her hand through the pile of groceries, and snagged my purse!

The worst part was, it was my own dumb fault! How could I have expected a pile of fruit snacks and juice boxes to completely hide my purse? With no other choice, I had to leave all the groceries behind and race to the preschool. The pitying glances of the people at the store—who couldn't help but feel sorry for the crazy pregnant lady—did not go unnoticed. It was enough to make me want to scream and cry, but there was no time for that. My preschooler was waiting!

So, what is the moral of this story? Honestly, I have no idea. Some days are just hard. You do the best you can with what you've got. Sometimes it turns out fine, but sometimes your purse gets stolen. Sometimes they recover it; sometimes they don't. Stuff happens. All we can do is put one foot in front of the other, make the best choices we can, and live with the outcome. And if it doesn't end well, we have no choice but to go home and have a cup of tea, throw ourselves into bed at night, and hope tomorrow is better. After all, you can't have your purse stolen two days in a row, can you?

Fortunately, no matter what kind of day we have, we can cling to this promise: "The steadfast love of the LORD never ceases; his mercies never come to an end; they are new every morning; great is your faithfulness" (LAMENTATIONS 3:22–23 ESV).

It's a good thing God's mercies are brand-new every morning. Otherwise, I don't think moms who are eight months pregnant, with a toddler in tow, would ever attempt grocery shopping again. So, my dear fellow moms, we have to realize that stuff happens—stuff that is completely out of our control. But we also need to realize that we can always count on the infinite mercies of God to get us through—with or without our purses!

—KAREN WILKERSON, BEDFORD, MASSACHUSETTS

Rejoicing in the Mess

*"Believe it or not, I started thanking God
for the mess and for allowing me to be
an imperfect mother with a perfect heavenly Father."*

God has blessed us with three biological children and one on the way. There are large gaps between their ages, but it's not because we planned it that way. It's because we struggle with fertility issues. Because of that, God led us to start fostering with a Christian nonprofit group. We've had almost a dozen extra blessings of all ages grace our home throughout the few years that we've been fostering. And the lessons the Lord has taught me through parenting are endless—even in the messiest of times.

We faced a most unfortunate set of circumstances when our middle child, Ryker, experienced major intestinal problems. Poor one-year-old Ryker woke up in the night with belly pain. The little guy barely went four hours without crying. Eventually, the screams began, indicating he was having a painful bowel movement. Thirty seconds later, the crying stopped. So, as sleep-deprived parents, we checked the monitor, saw that he was fine, and decided that since the crying had stopped it was in everyone's best interest that we go back to sleep. Sure enough, at 7:00 a.m., Ryker was awake, jumping in his bed, and oh, so happy. I took my time going into his room because he was so content. I made a quick breakfast, got the girls to the table, and then went to grab him.

Oh. My. Word.

Our happy little guy had had a major blowout—not only a blowout through the diaper, but a blowout through the zip-up sleeper. Let's just say that when enough pressure is placed on the zipper mechanisms, any solid (or liquid) will squish its way through, making spaghetti-like strings through the teeth of the zipper. It's gross, I know. But believe me when I tell you—there was poop EVERYWHERE! (Hold on, there's more.)

I put him in the tub, scrubbed him from head to toe, and finally had a clean, fresh-smelling boy. Being the "crunchy" mom that I am, I figured I might as well let him run free for a bit, sporting his ever-so-cute amber teething necklace and bare bottom. (He'd just pooped more poop than he had in a week, so he was surely cleaned out, right?)

While Ryker was playing and the girls were finishing their breakfast, I ran to clean the crib (and everything that had been within his reach). A few minutes later, I heard the girls putting their dishes in the sink. Then I heard a blood-curdling scream from Bryley, our oldest: "MOOOMMM! Ryker pooped on the floor!"

Okay, I thought. No biggie. I can handle it. I wrapped up cleaning the crib before I heard Bryley start to cry. *She must be overly concerned that I am taking so long,* I assumed. But when I saw what happened I instantly understood her tears. Ryker had indeed pooped on the floor—a strategically placed poop right where the girls were running. Bryley had slipped in it like she was sliding to home base. Had it been a softball game, the crowds would be cheering. Panic set in. How do I get her to the tub without making an even bigger mess?

I walked to the bathroom, holding her facing forward,

without her backside touching me and her leg in the air. It was then that she yelled, "He's pooping again!" Instinctively, I dropped her on the floor to grab Ryker. She fell on her bottom and started crying. I spun around to grab our poop machine and flung his bare bottom up, because, logically, with his bottom in the air nothing would fall on the floor, right? I didn't take into consideration that the poop had to go *somewhere*—it ended up in my just-washed hair and on the wall behind me. I held my baby upside down as my three-year-old foster daughter just stared at me. She looked unsure of what to do. Should she laugh? Should she cry? (Everyone else was!)

She looked at me with her big, brown eyes pondering the right move. And in that instance, with her worried eyes looking at me, I decided laughter, joy, and a thankful heart were the way to go. So, I sat down with a stinky, messy boy on my lap. I pulled my crying girl close and just laughed. Her cries turned to giggles, and we sat there laughing for several minutes. My sweet foster daughter kept her distance. (Can you blame her?) But at that moment, I showed her that even in the messiest of moments we can choose to laugh. Believe it or not, I started thanking God for the mess and for allowing me to be an imperfect mother with a perfect heavenly Father.

That experience reminds me of a song I sang as a child, a song based on Psalm 118:24, which says, "This is the day that the LORD has made; let us rejoice and be glad in it" (ESV). Never before had this verse meant so much to me!

God makes each day. Even the terrible, frustrating, days—He made them. I've learned to praise Him in those tough times, and by doing so, most days turn around for the better. My attitude helps my family and me get through.

Even through hard times, you can always find something to rejoice about. Rejoice in the Lord and all that He has given you. After all, a joyful heart is good medicine—even in the worst of messes.

—KALLIE SOMERS, MURFREESBORO, TENNESSEE

Giver of All Good Things

*"I made a choice to take all my hopes and dreams
and bundle them into one well-meaning heap.
I purposed to set them aside,
carefully tuck them away,
and trust God."*

Why do we procrastinate going to the grocery store? We wait until we're down to practically nothing before we finally load the kids in the car and head to the dreaded supermarket. Even when we buy in bulk—and pay in bulk—the supplies always run out and we start the cycle of dread all over again.

I'm a single mom who tries to go with the flow and make mundane tasks exciting. But sometimes, going with the flow becomes a tug-of-war—especially when large displays of superhero costumes are placed at the entrance of Costco.

My boys were the first to see them, and through their choruses of oohs and aahs, I tried to keep my mind focused on my grocery list. As luck would have it, a well-meaning sales clerk saw my boys' enthusiasm and casually mentioned that the costumes had just come in and would be the only shipment of costumes they would receive. Then she added that our timing was good because the costumes would soon be gone. You should have seen the look of panic on my boys' faces! Even though my children have been taught not to beg, their eyes pleaded all the words their mouths wanted to say.

After a short mental conversation with myself, I justified

the purchase. I knelt down to eye level and carefully explained to my boys that the costumes would be counted as one of their Christmas presents—not an *early* Christmas present but rather a present they got to open *on* Christmas.

With squeals, they jumped with joy and rushed to pick out the one they wanted. However, as we continued shopping, my eight-year-old began mulling things over in his mind. As we neared the register, his questions erupted. "Do we get to try them on? Can't we play with them before you wrap them? Why do we have to wait?" By the time we checked out, desperation had set in.

"Please, Mama, I *promise* I'll still be happy at Christmas!" he said, clutching the costume to his chest. "Please don't make me wait. I'll be *miserable*!" He even tried a bit of manipulation as he pulled away from me and gave me the look that said he was determined to do whatever necessary to break my will. His pleading continued until he was fighting back tears. Cupping his face in my hands, I tried reasoning with him. I explained that because we were buying it today, no other kids could snatch it up. The costume would be waiting for him to unwrap on Christmas morning.

"Doesn't it make you feel better knowing that?" I asked.

But he wasn't buying it. "No, Mama. That doesn't make me feel better! I can't wait!"

From past experience, I knew that reasoning with him was useless. So I knelt in front of him and laid out the law—and provided free entertainment for anyone shopping at Costco! I explained with sternness in my voice that I was buying the costume because he would really enjoy it. I loved him and wanted good things for him. I told him that on Christmas morning, as he unwrapped it, he'd be extremely thankful that he'd waited.

"Trust me," I finally said, closing the door on further arguments.

As we left the store, my boys chatted to one another, but my thoughts were far louder than their voices. I thought about the two words I'd said to my son, "Trust me," and realized how many times I'd failed to trust my heavenly Father.

For many years, I'd begged God for wholeness in my family. I'd asked for a man who would love my boys and be a wonderful dad to them, a man who would value God and family and be a partner for life. I'd reminded God that I could *never* be whole or happy without a complete family. I'd even tried to manipulate the Lord by fasting for days, all with the mentality that He might see my childish efforts and have pity on me. (Maybe He'd hurry and make things happen before I starved to death!) Oh, childish me.

As I realized the lesson that I'd just learned from my own child, I made a choice to take all my hopes and dreams and bundle them into one well-meaning heap. I purposed to set them aside, carefully tuck them away, and trust God. Just as I put those costumes away in the closet to save them for Christmas, I put my dreams aside for a future time. I don't have to fear. God has my future. Just as Trevor will open that present on Christmas morning and proclaim with joy that I was right, there *will* be a day when restoration comes to me. When it does, my joy will be boundless, and I'll be the first to proclaim that God was right.

In Isaiah 46:10, the Lord says, "I make known the end from the beginning, from ancient times, what is still to come. I say, 'My purpose will stand, and I will do all that I please'" (NIV). When I start to doubt God's timing, I have to remind myself of this verse. God's got this. He's got me.

Perhaps it would've been better to write this story after Christmas, when the gift was in Trevor's hands. But just like my own story, I've chosen to write it from the middle. I don't see the end, and neither does my son. I don't hold the gift yet and neither does he, but I am confident in the Giver of all good things. After all, He makes everything beautiful in His time.

—AMY DAVIS, KANSAS CITY, MISSOURI

No Kidding

*"God will cover you with His feathers,
and under His wings you will find refuge.
I cling to that in times of trouble."*

Lighthearted kidding and banter reigned at our house day in and day out when I was a new mom, so it was only natural for my younger kids—Jamie and Jon—to goof off no matter what life-altering event came our way. And we had many. Now, as a grandmother, my children's laughter still resounds in my ears.

Years ago, one day began with exhilaration as my family poured water into our water bottles. Everything else was packed in the car, ready for our Six Flags adventure.

"Mama, are you ready yet?" Jamie brushed her shoulder-length brown hair away from her eyes. To this day, I'll always remember the twinkle in her pale blue eyes.

I nodded and ushered Jon, the imp of the family, into the car. Within an hour from our Atlanta home, we arrived at the gate. We were ready for our yearly adventure!

At eleven years old, Little Miss Grown-up gathered her thick hair into a ponytail like a pro. I admired how she did everything with ease. She was my rock. Ever since I'd been diagnosed with arthritis a few years before, she was my right-hand gal. She laughed, joked, and cut up with me, yet also helped around the house. Jon was the one who teased me unmercifully. And my quiet husband, Jim, enjoyed it all.

All of us loved the excitement that the amusement park

brought. We loved the splashing sound of the logs as they hit the water with dripping wet, squealing kids waving at moms and dads. The roller coaster almost took our breath away but sent us into waves of laughter. And the dolphins! We all loved to watch them.

After walking the blazing, blacktopped streets for almost an hour, our faces dripped with perspiration from temps well above the midnineties. I wiped my forehead with the back of my hand. My head began to swim. I grabbed a nearby light pole to steady myself and rested a moment.

"Come on, Mom," the kids called. I wondered if my dizziness was hunger in disguise. After grabbing a slice of pizza, the wooziness returned. And then I began experiencing chest pains.

"Jim, I need to contact my doctor," I whispered.

Oblivious to my distress, my hubby waved at me. He turned toward the dolphin show that was already in progress. I saw the lithe animals explode into the air in a hail of water droplets. Jim stood watching the young woman throwing small fish to the dolphins. An expression of absolute joy filled his face.

Doesn't anyone take me seriously? I wondered.

Times were different then. We had never even heard of a cell phone. So, I found a pay phone and called my doctor. My doctor's tone was stern: "Get to the emergency room. Immediately!"

I caught up with Jim as the dolphin show ended. "I need to go to the emergency room."

"Why?" he asked as he grabbed my son by the hand and headed toward Thunder River. With my family, I learned you sometimes have to make things crystal clear.

"Because the doctor thinks I may be having a *heart attack*."

Jamie heard what I said but got between us anyway. "Are we going to ride Thunder River next?"

My family never takes me seriously. "Not right now, honey. I have to go to the hospital."

"Will you be long?" Jamie's blue eyes sparkled. Her ponytail swished as she turned to look at her dad for a positive response.

"No, we'll come back as soon as we can," I said.

We started toward the nearest exit. Right before we exited the park, the kids spotted a neat souvenir shop. "Oh please, Mama, just one souvenir?" Before I could answer, they raced into the store. Jim followed. I sat down on a brick wall, gasping for breath. I tried to look calm and collected, but inwardly I just hoped I wouldn't fall off the wall or that EMTs wouldn't rush me into an ambulance before they got back.

Soon, the kids ran outside with not one but two large whoopee cushions. *At least they're happy,* I thought.

In the front seat of the car, I held my hand over my racing heart, trying to still the irregular beats and counting the minutes until I could get help. The hospital was close to the amusement park, but it seemed like miles and miles. Especially after I heard "the noise," which rose to the height of depravity from the back seat—the most embarrassing sound I could think of. Then came the laughter of equally depraved children, squealing with glee.

I remember praying in all sincerity, "Lord, please don't let that be the last sound I hear before I die." The trip to the hospital, and annoying sounds, seemed to stretch on for hours. Fortunately, within several minutes, we arrived at the emergency room.

After completing forms, a nurse whisked me into a small

room where I was poked, prodded, and stuck by every available nurse. I had an abnormal EKG, and a nurse slipped nitro under my tongue.

The worry etched onto the nurses' faces told me they didn't think I would make it. With that thought firmly planted in my mind and growing roots, I weakly asked, "Could you please get my children? I want to see them. . ." I knew my children would be shocked at how bad off I was. A look of compassion grew in one nurse's brown eyes, and she immediately retrieved my children.

As I lay there, my life flashed on and off, much like Jim playing with the remote. First, I saw Jon as a little boy sitting on the kitchen floor, rolling his Hot Wheels to me or learning to ride his bike. I could see Jamie standing on a chair, helping me make gooey chocolate chip cookies and licking each of her fingers.

Jim looked grim as he and Jon walked in. Then Jamie walked over to my bed and touched my hand. *My poor little girl is so upset,* I thought. Jamie watched the nurse fiddle with my IV, and my little girl's eyes began to fill with tears. I wanted so badly to tell her God was with her and that He would protect me.

Jamie stood by my bed, her blue eyes swimming with crocodile tears. *My poor daughter,* I thought. *She's worried sick about me. God, what can I say to comfort her?* I knew that Psalm 91 says that God will cover you with His feathers, and under His wings you will find refuge. I cling to that in times of trouble.

Jamie looked at the wires protruding from me and back to the machine. And then to me. And before I could say a word, she said in a pained but clear voice, "Mama, does this mean we can't go back to Six Flags?"

I spent several days in the hospital, but everything turned out fine, with the exception of me having an abnormal EKG and heart arrhythmias. Jamie and Jon finally got over missing Six Flags, and to this day, we still laugh hysterically about it.

When I think back on this unfortunate-yet-funny event in my life, I'm reminded of Psalm 5:11: "But let all who take refuge in You be glad; let them ever sing for joy. Spread Your protection over them, that those who love Your name may rejoice in You" (NIV).

—NANETTE THORSEN-SNIPES, BUFORD, GEORGIA

Chocolate for Breakfast

"While I valued independence, personal choice, and 'letting things go,' my attitude reflected my own hang-ups and insecurities."

Nothing is impossible. This phrase is, perhaps, the mantra of every adventurous child. And to curate the creativity of that mindset, we parents often cater to their desire for possibility. However, while I yearn to be a "yes" mom, I'm armed against the freedom of indulgence that often breeds despair and disappointment.

Interestingly, Dutch children are reported to be happier than their international peers. Many Dutch children ride their bikes to school, play outside unsupervised, and even sell their own toys once a year during an annual holiday. In Dutch households, children may have chocolate sprinkles, or *hagelslag*, on their bread for breakfast each morning. This Dutch tradition reveals the mindset that if parents give their children more freedom, children will learn to moderate themselves.

While I have some Dutch blood in me, I don't offer chocolate sprinkles at breakfast. My seven-year-old doesn't ride his bike to school. My children's independent outdoor exploration is confined to our suburban backyard. And the thought of organizing a neighborhood garage sale so my children can sell their toys harrows my soul. So, what does all this mean for my children's mental confidence and emotional well-being?

Having studied early childhood play, I've taken one thing to heart: wherever there is a patch of earth, there is possibility for imagination. Personally, I want to foster the kind of space in which my kids are free to explore on their own terms. In taking a page from the Dutch parenting playbook, could my children create their own boundaries if I gave them a little room to explore? On the day I began to write this, my kids played on a patch of living room floor, not on a plot of land. Paper scraps were scattered across the room like colorful litter. However, instead of being stressed, when I walked into the room I said, "Creativity! Well-being! *Hagelslag!*"

However, my philosophy soon dissolved into an argument with my son about how he'd failed to clean up the paper scraps properly. The freedom I'd given hadn't helped my son construct healthy boundaries. In fact, he'd been thoughtless about the way he'd cleaned up the mess. He shoved paper in the closet without thought of the organized space around it. So, I did what any clever, God-fearing mom would do: I engaged in a five-minute discussion on the properties of the scrap-paper box, and I bookended the discussion nicely with a reenactment of how he'd done it wrong. I then reminded him that his paper-shoving habits revealed a general lack of effort that was showing up in other parts of his life. Nice. My actions completely contradicted the "free play" mindset I strive to foster.

It didn't take long before I realized the way I handled things didn't reflect the character of Jesus. My children *had* put the paper away, but because it wasn't the way I would have done it, it made me feel empty, sad, and like I'd failed as a human. My son's carelessness and lack of effort made me worry that his work ethic would hinder bigger jobs in life. While I valued independence, personal choice, and "letting things go," my attitude reflected my own hang-ups and insecurities. I showered my son with negative words, not because I cared about the paper but because I was overly concerned with raising responsible children.

As I pondered my feelings of failure, a *Mary Poppins Returns* phrase rattled around in my head: "You should never try to be the kind of person that you're not." It was so repetitive, I felt that God must have put it there. It made me ask the question, "How do I give my kids the freedom to err but still learn responsibility?"

First Corinthians 13:4 says, "Love is patient, love is kind. It does not envy, it does not boast, it is not proud" (NIV). Am I being prideful when I want my kids to do things in a way that meets my standard? Verse 5 goes on to say, "It does not dishonor others, it is not self-seeking, it is not easily angered, it keeps no record of wrongs." Sadly, I'd compared how my son put paper away to his entire character. Yes, I need to have clear expectations of my children, but my patience needs to outweigh my frustrations. I need to give my kids the room to make their choices rather than stand over them, judging their every move.

That same evening, my son and I had a heart-to-heart talk. I had been frustrated with him for not putting his best effort into several activities in his life, including horseback riding lessons and cleaning up at home. He explained to me that he was trying to do his best. I realized then that my expectations were too high and I was being too hard on him. I didn't like it that he wasn't doing things the way I wanted him to do them. He needed a little room to breathe.

I believe God wants us to create the kind of rules that preserve us, not inhibit us. Our children will make the connections between the lessons we teach and the freedoms we give, but we must be patient with them and not expect too much out of them. After all, God is patient with us. He loves us. And because of Jesus' death, we are forgiven for every parenting imperfection.

At the end of the day, our confidence in our Father's love is an extraordinary gift, and showing God's love is what breeds well-being in our families. Our children—and their parents—are "fearfully and wonderfully made" (PSALM 139:14 NIV). We want to set healthy expectations for our kids without being too hard on them. If that means giving them chocolate for breakfast—at least every once in a while—then so be it.

—DEBRA MCGOLDRICK, DOWNERS GROVE, ILLINOIS

When You Don't Know
What to Do

*"When we ask Him, God grants wisdom
that is worthy of our obedience."*

"Mom, I have a problem."

It's the phone greeting no one wants. For a parent, those five words have the power to rev up the circulatory system and unleash a maximum dose of adrenaline.

It was a gorgeous day, and with nothing on the calendar, my son had gone fishing. He drove our four-wheeler to the nearby shoreline to see if anything was biting. He'd been gone a couple hours when I received his call. Before he had a chance to elaborate, I felt the blood drain from my face and dump into my heart. I froze. A litany of horrible possibilities rolled through my mind like movie credits. Was a fishhook lodged in his lip? Had he broken his leg? Had someone drowned? I waited for him to deliver the worst possible news.

"I lost the four-wheeler key."

All my bodily systems began to return to normal, and I was left with an extreme case of emotional whiplash.

"How long have you been looking for it?" I asked, relieved that he was okay.

"About forty-five minutes."

That's a solid effort for a teenage boy, and I could hear his worry and discouragement. I drove the two minutes to his location, where he was slumped on the parked four-wheeler, and I began my investigation. We retraced his steps as best we could through tall, dry grass laid down by recently melted snowdrifts. We tromped through mud—the kind that stinks and makes a sucking noise every time you take a step. A few minutes into our key-finding mission, I realized our efforts were futile. The area was too vast, and every square inch was the perfect hiding place for a tiny key.

If we didn't find the key, though, he would bear the responsibility for the loss, the shame of telling his brothers, and perhaps the expense of installing a new ignition or making a new key. So, I did what I do when I have no idea what to do. I told the Lord about it. "Lord, this is impossible. If we are going to find that key, You will have to show us where it is."

My son half walked, half moped two steps behind me. I wondered if he had been praying for help, but I hesitated to ask him. If I suggested we ask God to help us find the key and then we didn't find it, I'd feel obligated to explain God's ways. I might even feel embarrassed that God didn't come through for us. But what if we did find it? That would be nothing short of a miracle. If we prayed for help from the start, we would know God had heard and answered.

This mental wrestling match went on for several minutes when a third option came to mind: What if we asked God and did not find the key? We would have the opportunity to reflect on God's goodness even when things don't turn out as we hoped.

When my boys were young, I hung a framed poster of James 1:5 in their room. It looked like a WANTED poster from an old Western movie, and it read, "If any of you lacks wisdom, he should ask God, who gives to all generously and without criticizing, and it will be given to him" (JAMES 1:5

HCSB). Hanging the leftover VBS decoration in their room was my stealthy plan to help them hide God's Word in their hearts. It hung on the wall facing their beds. When they fell asleep and woke up, they'd see that verse. I hoped that over time, it would be imprinted on their minds. But God did something stealthy Himself. He used that poster to cement that Scripture in my heart.

When James wrote those words to believers, he wasn't offering a providential formula. He qualified his statement by stating that when we ask God for wisdom, we must "believe and not doubt" (JAMES 1:6 NIV). For many years, I thought that sounded a lot like wishing on a star. If I believed sincerely, then God would grant my wish. But James wasn't writing about granting wishes. He was writing about gaining wisdom. When we ask God for wisdom, we must "believe and not doubt" that the wisdom He generously gives is good and trustworthy. When God grants wisdom through His Word, His Spirit, or His people, we demonstrate belief by actively heeding it.

Sometimes, when God gives wise direction, I wait around kicking the gravel because I can't decide if He's trustworthy. That's asking with doubt. I do not merely doubt that He'll grant my wish. I also doubt His goodness. And that says more about me than it does about God. Is God good when you're in the ER having a fishhook removed from your face? Is God good when you have to empty your piggy bank to pay for a new key? Is God really good all the time? He is. And He is good in the most surprising ways. He doesn't promise to grant my wish. He promises to grant wisdom that will guide me through the weeds of life.

I finally asked my son, "Have you asked the Lord to help?"

"Yes," he replied, and I felt relieved.

We hiked up bluffs and down onto the muddy shoreline

until the lake lapped against a shale cliff and we could go no farther. "Did you go anywhere else?" I asked him.

"I climbed up this cliff, but I fell down." He pointed to the spot, "If I dropped it here, it's probably buried under all this crumbled rock."

We clawed our way up the cliff, and with every movement of forward progress, we created an avalanche of shale. If the key had been up there, it was surely at the bottom by now. I began to rake through the loose shale with my fingers, back and forth, taking a swath as wide as my arms could reach. I told my son to do the same.

Ten seconds later, I was holding the key.

Sometimes I wonder if God is listening. And sometimes I want to fall on my face because I had the audacity to wonder. God created us and loves us and listens to us. When we ask Him, God grants wisdom that is worthy of our obedience.

Losing four-wheeler keys may seem worthy of an eye roll, not a prayer. When people around me are suffering from much bigger problems, it feels strange to trouble God— as if that were possible—with my seemingly insignificant problems. But I do it anyway. In more serious matters, I have asked the Lord for help and found myself still raking through shale, with nothing more than a handful of dirt to show for my asking.

We can't explain God's timing or His purpose, but we can trust His goodness. Though we may not understand His plan in our suffocating struggle, God is not confused or blinded. If He sees when a hair falls from a head, when a sparrow falls to the ground, and when a four-wheeler key falls into the shale, then we can trust His goodness and wisdom in all things, all the time.

— SHAUNA LETELLIER, PIERRE, SOUTH DAKOTA

Embracing the Mess

*"I've learned that if my eyes are focused on my plans
and not on Jesus, I will inevitably be discouraged."*

I've been a parent for several years now, and in that time my husband and I have definitely had our share of challenges. One of the most stressful challenges we've taken on as parents is traveling with our kiddos.

Our first trip, when our oldest daughter was six months old, took us to a family wedding in New Orleans. Navigating the airport and the flight was surprisingly a breeze—despite balancing an active baby across our laps for two hours while also trying to assemble some sort of privacy while nursing. I battled the obstacles once we finally arrived, including traversing a new city with a sleep-deprived infant by myself while my husband attended his best man duties. And Bourbon Street with a baby? Not exactly kid-friendly.

When our second daughter joined our family, we braved a fifteen-hour cross-country car ride with a toddler and infant in tow (my ears are *still* ringing from all the crying). Still, the challenges of the trip didn't end when the car stopped and our feet hit the sand. I've realized when it comes to traveling, the journey itself isn't usually the most challenging part. It's the twists and turns we experience once we actually reach our destination.

Our most memorable vacation (is *vacation* the right word when kids are involved?) was our trip to Florida when my eldest was nine months old. It was February. We had been cooped up inside while enduring the Chicago winter for three long months, and the warmth of the Florida sun on our faces made us feel brand-new. I watched my baby physically and mentally transform into a functioning, opinionated, independent human—almost overnight. She was starting to show her adventurous side, embracing life outside of our typical routine. About halfway through our trip we were invited to go on a six-hour boat ride. We'd be overlapping nap time, sitting in the sun all day, and—doing the one activity dreaded by all newish parents—eating out at a restaurant. The thought of containing an overtired infant in the middle of a hot, crowded restaurant made me break out into a cold sweat. The nap time warden in me wanted to hold back, but my daughter's new anything-goes-we're-on-vacation attitude inspired me, and we embarked on our first boating adventure as a family. I made sure her outfit was Instagram-worthy, from the strappy baby sandals to the floppy beach hat. And the day was pretty much perfect.

Until lunch.

We had stopped at a quirky waterfront eatery, a favorite of our hosts, to grab a bite before turning around and heading back to the marina. Despite only napping a total of ten minutes on the boat, my daughter was taking the going-out-to-eat experience like a champ. She was all smiles as the servers and patrons walked by. She ate her cut-up strawberries like no one's business. Up to this point my husband and I had heeded the advice given by veteran parents on taking their children out to eat. We had decided it wouldn't be worth the hassle, but now our nine-month-old was showing us we had nothing to fear. This was a piece of cake!

When burgers and fries were all gone, it was time to get back on the boat. I started to pick up the inevitably dropped strawberries on the floor when I saw the reason my nine-month-old was so full of smiles. It was all over the high chair and all over the restaurant floor. I'll spare you any additional visual imagery—it's enough to say that this mess (and the smell) was unlike any other I'd experienced as a mom. Our outing had taken a sharp turn, with me racing with the baby to the changing room, emerging almost forty minutes later with both of our formerly Instagram-worthy outfits a little worse for the wear. Needless to say, I was more than grateful when we got back to the marina and I could finally get back to the hotel and take a shower.

A few years have passed since our first boat ride and restaurant adventure/fiasco, and countless other experiences have played out very differently in real life than I had imagined them in my head. As moms, we quickly learn that plans go awry and life is messy. My attempts to take on new adventures, even an everyday trip across town to a new playground, remind me that life throws us curveballs and our plans are not always the best plans for us.

I've learned that if my eyes are focused on my plans and not on Jesus, I will inevitably be discouraged. In those moments, I need to remember that God knows our future plans, but that doesn't mean the future won't have its messes. When my plans don't go the way I envisioned, I'm reminded of Proverbs 19:21, which says, "Many are the plans in a person's heart, but it is the LORD's purpose that prevails" (NIV). I'm also reminded of Isaiah 55:8, where God says, "My thoughts are not your thoughts, neither are your ways My ways" (NIV).

I'm so thankful I can look back on that first restaurant experience and laugh about it. That day I learned I had to be flexible as a parent, and I learned to let go of my control and let life happen. We had a great afternoon with friends, saw several dolphins jumping in the waves, and saw our daughter's face light up the first time she felt the sand between her toes. Perhaps those were the plans God had for us on that day—to enjoy God's creation and learn from Him in both its beauty and its messes.

—KELLY COLLINS, WHEATON, ILLINOIS

The Heart's Desires

"I had no idea how God would rearrange my life and, in the process, fulfill one of my heart's desires."

About five years ago, God put it on our hearts to become foster parents. Like any mom, I was filled with reservations and doubts about my mothering ability. My husband has four biological kids, the youngest of them a thirteen-year-old daughter who was living with us. I have two biological kids, the youngest a fifteen-year-old son who was living with us. We felt it would be important for our kids at home to see the needs of foster kids and grow in their compassion for others. We were not prepared for the impact fostering would have on us—the good, bad, ugly, and many times very emotional sides of this journey.

Shortly after the ink was dry on our foster license, I received a call from a friend who had been a foster parent for a few years. During the conversation, she mentioned a little boy who needed a home. He had a deadly disease and was totally deaf. I couldn't believe it! After high school graduation, I attended college in hopes of becoming an interpreter for the deaf. I only went for a year and didn't graduate, but I kept up with sign language through the years at church and with friends. I immediately knew this was our kid. After a few calls and some work behind the scenes, he came to live with us. I was so nervous but sure beyond any doubt that this was God's confirmation that we were following His plan.

We quickly realized this adorable little two-year-old was

going to challenge every parenting skill we thought we had. He had zero language and communicated with hitting, biting, scratching, and lighting up the room with gigantic smiles and little excited jumps. As much as I wanted to start teaching him sign language, our first challenge was to get him healthy. He had sickle cell disease and had to be on daily meds. Any attempt to get the sticky, liquid meds down his throat resulted in fierce refusal. This twice-daily struggle took both my husband and me—one to hold him and the other to figure out how to trick him into allowing the meds down his throat. The result was two frazzled parents, faces covered in a mix of sticky penicillin and toddler spit, and a self-satisfied toddler with less than half his dose in his belly.

After the initial hurdle of getting his body started on healthy foods and medicine, we were able to begin to focus on sign language. We noticed immediately that he was very smart. He could mimic any sign and would notice the slightest change in facial expressions. When he was in the room, I would sign every object, sign directions repeatedly, and make sure he was looking directly at me when communicating.

A few weeks went by and we finally had our aha moment. He loved to turn the light switch on and off but was too short to reach it. He would stand under the light switch, reach up, and cry out, "Ahh, ahh." Then I would sign "light please," and then pick him up and let him flip the switch. One day, he wanted to turn on the light, so I signed it and he mimicked my sign, then pointed to the light again. After much praise, he ran back over and signed it again, then pointed. Again, much praise, and he understood that these hand signals meant he could use the switch. He tried it multiple times that day with the same result every time. He was thrilled!

The next day, he started with the switch again and then brought me into the kitchen by my hand and signed "banana" and pointed at the counter. Previously, we would spend quite some time trying to figure out what he wanted by pointing and crying and pointing and crying and frustrations rising. This time, though, I handed him the banana, and his smile was brighter than all the lights in the house! He proceeded to do a little happy dance all around the kitchen. He used his hands to ask for something, and he got it. Wow, what a happy day! From that moment, his little mind was a sponge. He would sit on the couch with little alphabet/picture blocks and pick them up one at a time, asking for the sign. He finally had a way to communicate. This was one of the most precious experiences I had ever had as a mom.

So many dreams seem to die when we don't finish college or our lives turn in unexpected directions. But God has a plan for us. I did not know the Lord when I left for college straight out of high school. But college is where I first placed my faith and trust in Him; that's where I began to see a different possibility, a new way of living. As the years passed, I gave up my dream of being an interpreter. I still loved the language but knew I did not have the skills or the physical ability to handle this physically demanding job. It sort of became a hobby as I signed music in church or home and taught my kids the basics so I could tell them no across the room without raising my voice. I had no idea how God would rearrange my life and, in the process, fulfill one of my heart's desires. Since then, we've adopted our little guy and he is doing amazing!

God knows our hopes and dreams. "The LORD directs the steps of the godly. He delights in every detail of their lives" (PSALM 37:23 NLT). God does not waste anything. He knows you inside and out and knows your heart better than you do.

—JOSIE ELLISTON, BROCK, TEXAS

Kitty Litter Confetti

"I was convinced I would destroy my children's pure and happy hearts. Surely, I would fail as a single parent!"

In order for you to comprehend the extent of my downfall, I must first describe to you the serious rock-star heights to which I'd ascended. My husband, Clint, had been battling cancer for nearly two years, and during the unexpected timing of his decline and death, a church in Rochester, Minnesota, hired me as a ministry coordinator. Experts suggest *not* making life-altering decisions in the throes of grief—but I made them all.

Five days following my husband's memorial service, I embarked on a two-week road trip with three girls under the age of ten. We had two tents, two cats, three bikes, and everything else you could imagine. Why the cats, you ask? I took them because people had bent over backward for our family during my husband's illness, and I was tired of asking for favors. Also, I was amped up on adrenaline and numbed by an overdose of emotional novocaine. I'd not yet felt the impact of my husband's death, but still I felt separation anxiety seeping in. So, it was no cat left behind!

We began our road trip and my steady ascent toward the title of "Rock Star Mom." The status rivaled sainthood, really. First, I drove past our new home in Rochester to show the girls where they'd be living, and then we paid a visit to the World's Largest Truck Stop in Iowa. Then we went to the Gateway Arch in St. Louis before stopping in Evansville, Indiana—a must for the Evanses!

The Louisville Slugger Museum offered free sex education, literally embodied in a golden, thirty-foot David statue. My kids sat at a bus stop, staring up at David, attempting to comprehend the meaning of life. (I kept thinking how convenient it was that my husband decided to bail for the inevitable conversation that followed.)

We snapped selfies at Asbury Theological Seminary, where Clint had received his Master of Divinity. We camped in Huntington, West Virginia, and took a really long shortcut in Colonial Williamsburg (in 98-degree weather). Then we arrived at a campsite on Chincoteague Island in Virginia— one week before the famous annual Pony Swim. I had even purchased a book on CD so we could listen to the fictional story of the Assateague Island ponies (while driving to see the actual Assateague Island ponies).

It felt like angels were singing the "Hallelujah Chorus" as light shone down from heaven and cherubs donned me with my glimmering, red, rock star cape. My heroic daughters presented me with their best efforts to "help" set up the campsite. In the end, they chased each other like lunatics while I finished raising our tents. By the time I'd organized our gear, sweat soaked through my clothes and strands of my hair were vacuum-sealed to my forehead. But despite my grime-coated skin, I felt satisfaction of a job well done.

I showered faster than a speeding bullet, and even with the humidity, I felt cool and clean sitting at the picnic table with my road atlas, charting the next steps of our course. I looked at my oldest daughter beside me, reading a book, and my youngest daughters laughing happily in the van and thought, *Maybe single parenting won't be so bad. These girls are amazing humans.*

I had nearly forgotten our family's great sadness and had decided to take the girls out for pizza. My phone was charging in the van, so I slowly unfolded from the picnic table and sauntered over to the car. Grinning, I opened the minivan door. My girls' giggles died immediately and my rock star–mom grin vanished.

I hate to admit this, but I used words I swore I would never speak in front of my children, much less *at* them. One of the cats named Patter had emerged from his litter box covered in kitty litter. My girls, thinking the sight hilarious, had concurred a simple equation: more kitty litter equals more hilarity. Their angelic laughter had been spurred on by throwing dirty—DIRTY—litter on both of the cats like celebration confetti. As Pitter and Patter dodged the fanfare by shimmying into all corners of the car, my entire van was covered with cat urine and feces. There was urine-soaked sand in my icy drink, my purse, on the clothes, pillows, and snack bag. It was even in an open jar of peanut butter! (Why, oh why, was there an open jar of peanut butter?)

I screamed at my girls. I shamed them. I shouted until my throat was raw. I cannot remember ever pitying myself more than I did in that moment. Then, without warning, my shrieking morphed into tears of frustration followed by sobs of guilt. Eventually, the three of us fell into a heap of blubbering, emotional females.

As I cradled my wailing children, tears streaked down my face and splashed into their hair. Clint had been so much more patient with them. I was convinced I would destroy my children's pure and happy hearts. Surely, I would fail as a single parent!

Eventually, I regained my inner adult. I apologized to a neighboring family for my behavior— and apologized to my own children. I drove to a gas station and instructed the girls to clean out the car. Ninety minutes later, we parked a newly vacuumed van in the parking lot of a pizza place. The road trip had survived my raging outburst.

One year and multiple minivan cleanings later, I still find bits of kitty litter and cringe. But when I ask my girls what they remember most about the road trip, they say things like "visiting family, going to Chocolate World, and seeing New York City." Each time they speak of our adventure, their faces light up with the vibrance of one of our memories.

Their grace for me, the mom who lost it on that trip, reminds me of Lamentations 3:22–23: "Because of the LORD's great love we are not consumed, for His compassions never fail. They are new every morning; great is Your faithfulness" (NIV).

When I consider this verse in light of the kitty-litter confetti, I see God's love for me reflected in my own children. When they said, "We forgive you, Mom. We love you," they meant it. To them, forgiven means forgotten. Sounds a lot like God's love and forgiveness, doesn't it? "As far as the east is from the west, so far has He removed our transgressions from us" (PSALM 103:12 NIV).

We can recite each chapter and verse of all our Great Parent Failures, but God shakes His head at us and says, "Nope. My mercies are new every morning." That's the wonderful part of being God's children. We are fiercely loved. And just as our sweet children forgive us, our heavenly Father forgives us too. But we need to remember to forgive ourselves. We cannot maintain rock star–mom status 100 percent of the time. And, as God's mercy reminds us, that's okay.

—SAMANTHA EVANS, ROCHESTER, MINNESOTA

LIVE YOUR FAITH

Dear Friend,

This book was prayerfully crafted with you, the reader, in mind. Every word, every sentence, every page was thoughtfully written, designed, and packaged to encourage you—right where you are this very moment. At DaySpring, our vision is to see every person experience the life-changing message of God's love. So, as we worked through rough drafts, design changes, edits, and details, we prayed for you to deeply experience His unfailing love, indescribable peace, and pure joy. It is our sincere hope that through these Truth-filled pages your heart will be blessed, knowing that God cares about you—your desires and disappointments, your challenges and dreams.

He knows. He cares. He loves you unconditionally.

BLESSINGS!
THE DAYSPRING BOOK TEAM

Additional copies of this book and
other DaySpring titles can be purchased
at fine retailers everywhere.
Order online at <u>dayspring.com</u>
or
by phone at 1-877-751-4347